REPUTATIONS

HITLER

Nathaniel Harris

B.T. BATSFORD LTD, LONDON

Typeset by Tek-Art Ltd, Kent
and printed in Great Britain by
The Bath Press, Bath
for the publishers
B.T. Batsford Ltd
4 Fitzhardinge Street
London W1H 0AH

ISBN 0 7134 5961 1

Acknowledgments

The Author and Publishers would like to thank
the following for kind permission to reproduce
illustrations in this book: Barnaby's Picture
Library for pages 6(a), 12, 13, 31(a), 31(b), 36, 37,
40(b), 42, 60; Mary Evans Picture Library for
pages 33, 39(a), 39(b), 50; The Robert Hunt
Library for page 15; The Imperial War Museum
for page 9, and Popperfoto for pages 10, 11, 16,
17(a), 17(b), 19, 26, 29, 41, 43, 47, 49, 58. The map
on page 14 was drawn by Robert Brien

Frontispiece *Hitler leads, others follow.*

Cover Illustrations (*top left*) Hitler meets
Chamberlain and Mussolini at the Munich
conference (courtesy Popperfoto); (*top right*) An
offical portrait of Hitler (courtesy Mary Evans
Picture Library); (*bottom right*) Hitler in the
Sudetenland, 1938 (courtesy Popperfoto); (*bottom
left*) Third Reich postage stamps (courtesy
Barnaby's Picture Library); (*left*) Hitler reviews
the German fleet (courtesy Popperfoto).

Contents

Time Chart

1889   Adolf Hitler born at Braunau in Austria.

1905   Hitler leaves school.

1907   Hitler fails to gain a place in the Vienna Academy of Fine Arts.

1907-13   Hitler lives in Vienna, from 1909 in a men's hostel.

1913   Hitler moves to Munich in Bavaria (Germany).

1914   Outbreak of First World War; Hitler enlists in German Army.

1916   Hitler wounded.

1917   Russian Revolution.

1918   Hitler awarded the Iron Cross, First Class. Temporarily blinded by British gas attack, he is hospitalized in Germany. First World War ends with defeat of Germany. Kaiser abdicates; Germany becomes a republic (the Weimar Republic).

1919   Post-war Versailles settlement imposes harsh terms on Germany. In Munich, Hitler is employed as a political agent by the army; he joins the tiny new German Workers' Party, soon to become the Nazi Party. Fascist Party founded in Italy.

1920   Hitler leaves the army and begins to make the Nazi Party a force in Bavarian politics.

1921   Hitler acquires dictatorial powers within the Nazi Party.

1922   Mussolini and Fascists come to power in Italy after the 'March on Rome'.

1923   French occupy Ruhr. Massive inflation disrupts German life and economy. Hitler's 'Beer-Hall Putsch' fails.

1924   Hitler sentenced to five years' imprisonment, but released in November. In prison, begins to dictate *Mein Kampf*.

1925   Ban on Nazi Party lifted. First volume of *Mein Kampf* published. International tension relaxes after signing of Locarno Pact.

1929   Hitler becomes nationally known in campaign against Young Plan. Wall Street Crash heralds world-wide Depression.

1930   Depression begins to be felt in Germany. Nazis poll six million votes in general election.

1931   Japan annexes Manchuria.

1932   Nazis poll 13 million votes and become largest political party, but experience setback in November general election.

1933   Hitler becomes German chancellor. Reichstag fire gives Nazis excuse to impose state of emergency. Nazis poll 43.9 per cent of votes in new election. Political parties and trade unions dissolved; Germany becomes totalitarian state.

1934   'Night of the Long Knives' eliminates SA (stormtroopers) as a political force. Hitler combines offices of president and chancellor. Germany withdraws from League of Nations, concludes non-aggression pact with Poland. Austrian Nazis stage coup which fails.

1935   Conscription introduced in Germany. Anglo-German Naval Agreement. Italians conquer Abyssinia.

1936   German troops occupy Rhineland. Outbreak of Spanish Civil War. German-Italian 'Axis'.

1937   Japanese invade China.

1938   Anschluss (union) of Austria and Germany. Munich agreement: large areas of Czechoslovakia ceded to Germany. 'Crystal Night': anti-Jewish pogrom.

1939   Fascists victorious in Spanish Civil War. Hitler arranges dismemberment of Czechoslovakia. Italian conquest of Albania. German-Italian 'Pact of Steel'. Nazi-Soviet non-aggression pact. Germany attacks Poland. Britain and France declare war on Germany.

1940   Germans invade and conquer Norway, Denmark, Holland, Belgium and France. Italians enter war on German side. RAF victorious in the 'Battle of Britain'.

1941   Germany attacks USSR. Japan attacks American Pacific Fleet at Pearl Harbor; Hitler and Mussolini also declare war on USA.

1942   Beginning of mass gassings of Jews, Gypsies etc. by the Nazis. Axis forces driven from North Africa.

1943   Catastrophic German defeats in Russia. Allied invasion of Italy; fall of Mussolini.

1944   Allied landings in Normandy (D-Day). Failure of 'July plot' to assassinate Hitler.

1945   Invasion of Germany. Hitler commits suicide. Unconditional surrender of Germany. Two atomic bombs dropped on Japan, which surrenders. End of Second World War.

The Reputation

An Evil Reputation

'I shall go down in history as the greatest German!' exclaimed a delighted Adolf Hitler in 1939, after adding Austria and Czechoslovakia to his dominions. Then, in the following year, he was hailed as 'the greatest War Lord of all time' when his armies mastered the Continent. Millions of people would have agreed with these descriptions of Hitler at this moment, when his ultimate defeat and downfall seemed unthinkable. Later, many others would go to the opposite extreme and argue that he was a mediocrity with nothing remarkable about him except the crudity of his ideas and the brutality with which he put them into effect. Few reputations have oscillated so violently within a few decades, or generate such fierce passions whenever a historian questions established views on the subject.

Whatever personal qualities Hitler may or may not have possessed, there is no denying the extraordinary nature of his career. Austrian by birth, in the 1920s he emerged from obscurity to make his National Socialist (Nazi) party a force in German politics. In 1933 he took power, establishing himself as dictator and turning Germany into a one-party state. With Hitler as its Führer, the country overcame its economic depression and recovered the great power status it had lost after being defeated in the First World War. Abroad, Hitler won large territories for Germany by a spectacularly successful policy of bluff and threats, but without firing a shot. When his invasion of Poland finally led to the outbreak of the Second World War in 1939, his armies rapidly defeated France; and the survival of Britain, his sole remaining enemy, seemed irritating rather than dangerous. In 1941, having launched an apparently successful assault against Soviet Russia, Hitler found himself the master of a vast continental empire.

Führer: German word for 'Leader'.

But this proved to be the end of his good fortune. The Russians fought back, the United States entered the war on the Anglo-Russian side, and the overwhelming strength of this combination ensured the defeat of Germany. Shortly before the end, Hitler killed himself, leaving Europe in ruins and tens of millions dead.

This was an extraordinary career on several counts – the scale of Germany's conquests and catastrophes, the unbridled power acquired by her Leader, and also the unparalleled way in which that power was justified and used. Everything was done in the name of doctrines such as no state had ever before adopted – that the Germans were a racially superior people, that the Jews were their sworn enemies, and that most other peoples were sub-human 'cattle' whose destinies should be determined by the Germanic 'master race'. In the struggle between races, all means were legitimate; humanity and compassion were no more than symptoms of weakness. And so a fearful, boastful barbarism characterized Hitler's regime from first to last, culminating in the ruthless exploitation of slave labour, organized mass murder, and frightful reprisals against any who dared to resist.

The twentieth century has produced a large crop of horrors – large enough to have shaken the confidence in human progress that was so common only a hundred years ago. But Nazism remains a uniquely appalling episode in modern history because its atrocities were premeditated, executed with the latest technological expertise, and glorified as expressions of health and strength of purpose.

In view of these facts, Hitler and Hitlerism are likely to stand condemned during the foreseeable future. Moreover Hitler can be said to have been 'wrong' even in terms of his own philosophy, which recognized no moral law but strength ('might is right'), since he failed. At a fundamental level – a judgement about good and evil, right and wrong – Hitler's reputation is no longer a subject of controversy.

However, to dismiss Hitler as 'evil', or 'a monster' does not do much to advance our understanding of the man or his career. When we get down to details – questions about Hitler's aims, the quality of his leadership, the significance of his decisions – we find that the historians of Nazism disagree profoundly among themselves. Was Hitler a frenzied rabble-rouser, or was he in fact a cool calculator? Did he dominate events or take his cue from them? Were his foreign policies radically different from those of German statesmen before him? Did he want war or blunder into it? Did he direct the war well or badly? How responsible was he for the Nazis' most infamous crime, the annihilation of the Jews? Did he lose touch with reality, or was he sane (or mad) all the way through his career? Evidently there are good reasons for taking another look at his reputation.

Images of a dictator. (Left) The strong man. (Right) Ailing and failing at the end, as he decorates the young boys sent out to defend the tottering Reich.

The Background

The Era of World Wars

Young Hitler's world: races and nations in conflict

Adolf Hitler grew up before the First World War in a country that no longer exists – the multi-national empire of Austria-Hungary, ruled by the Habsburg dynasty. Like other monarchs, the Habsburgs were faced with problems such as industrialization, the introduction of a parliamentary system and the growth of socialism; but the most intractable of their problems was one specific to Austria-Hungary – the mixture of Germans, Hungarians, Czechs, Slovaks, Poles, Croats, Slavs, Slovenes, Italians and other increasingly national-minded ethnic groups that co-existed uneasily within the borders of the empire. The dynasty had only survived by delicate balancing, making judicious concessions or playing one nation off against another.

Given this background, Hitler's fanatical German nationalism and racism becomes comprehensible – especially since he spent his young manhood in the cosmopolitan capital of the empire, Vienna, where ethnic antagonisms and racist ideas were particularly in evidence. In fact most of the central doctrines of Nazism were not invented by Hitler, but were picked up by him in pre-war Vienna from pamphlets and political meetings.

Hitler's belief that the Germans were racially superior to the Slavs and other peoples was also based on real historical events, even if he drew the wrong conclusions from them. As well as a tendency to expand their area of settlement, the Germans had for centuries penetrated deep into Eastern Europe as traders, bringing with them a more sophisticated culture than that of the peasant peoples among whom they settled. It was chiefly thanks to German commercial colonists that towns grew up, and many of these remained German enclaves in otherwise non-German territories. Understandably, Germans often flattered themselves on performing a historic 'civilizing' mission in respect of their eastern neighbours, and were tempted to believe that they were inherently superior to them – a conviction that Hitler was to share and exploit.

Hitler was least original of all in his hatred of the Jews. By his own account he acquired this in Vienna, where anti-semitism was rife; but by that time, of course, it was centuries old. In Europe, anti-semitism had begun with the belief that the Jews were 'Christ killers', but their consequent persecution created new reasons for hating them. They kept themselves separate from Christians – and were kept separate by being made to live in ghettoes and wear badges that instantly identified them as Jews. Restricted to a few trades, including the highly unpopular one of money-lending, they displayed an industriousness that is typical of minority groups under pressure – and provokes the envy and irritation of the unpressured majority. Like other minorities, they served as scapegoats who could be blamed for a variety of ills by governments in difficulties, and,

When, for example, the Habsburgs found it impossible to rule solely by relying on their German subjects, they made the Hungarians partners in the running of the empire. Hence in 1867 the former Austrian Empire became Austria-Hungary.

Can you think of any similar minorities, past or present?

since they were constantly driven from one country to the next, the Jews remained 'foreigners' almost everywhere, and as such an object of dislike and suspicion.

For these reasons anti-semitism failed to disappear quickly even in the nineteenth century, when the growth of gentile tolerance was paralleled by a tendency for Jews in western and central Europe to become integrated into the national communities. In some quarters this merely stimulated fears that the Jews were 'taking over' or in some mysterious fashion corrupting and ruining the country; for those who wished to believe it, a famous forged document, *The Protocols of the Elders of Zion*, revealed the existence of a concerted Jewish conspiracy to control the world. Anti-semitism played a major role in the famous Dreyfus affair in France, and racist stereotypes of Jews were commonplace in English writing until the Second World War.

Nevertheless, an intelligent observer would have said that anti-semitism was on the wane in civilized countries such as Britain, France and Germany – though not in backward Russia, where, during Hitler's boyhood, the Tsar was trying to divert popular discontent from the autocracy by encouraging pogroms – violent attacks on Jewish communities – in the belief that he could 'drown the revolution in Jewish blood'.

It follows that Hitler's anti-semitism, like his other nationalist and racist convictions, was not a merely personal aberration. What could not have been predicted was that a man holding such convictions would become the chosen leader of a clever, cultivated, 'advanced' people. And indeed, but for the trauma of the First World War and its aftermath, it is unlikely that such a thing could ever have happened.

The World War and after

In 1913, a year before the outbreak of war, Hitler left Austria-Hungary and settled in the south German province of Bavaria. Imperial Germany, with Kaiser Wilhelm II at its head, was the most powerful state in Europe, possessing a formidable army that was perceived as a threat by France in particular. As a result, the firm partnership between Germany and Austria-Hungary was countered by a Franco-Russian alliance. Britain too was drawn into understandings with France and Russia, and by the early years of the twentieth century Europe was divided into two rapidly arming camps.

Then, on 28 June 1914, the assassination of the Austrian Archduke Franz Ferdinand at Sarajevo sparked off a Balkan crisis which revived Austro-Russian rivalry in the region. Each state was backed up by its allies, and a series of diplomatic exchanges, mobilizations and counter-mobilizations escalated into an all-out war. Germany, Austria-Hungary and Turkey (the Central Powers) fought on one side; Russia, France and Britain (the Entente) on the other. Historians continue to disagree about who was responsible for actually starting the war. All that need be said here is that at the time the Entente powers were entirely convinced of Germany's 'war-guilt', while the Germans were equally convinced of their innocence.

The Great War of 1914-18 was immeasurably more terrible than any previous conflict. On the Western Front, millions died in the muddy trenches of northern France, and many other soldiers, including Corporal Adolf Hitler, were wounded or gassed. In the East, though somewhat different in character, the war was equally hard fought, the Russians and Austrians in particular suffering some catastrophic reverses; and in 1915 a third, Alpine front opened up when Italy joined the Entente and began hostilities against Austria-Hungary.

In 1894 a Jewish officer, Captain Alfred Dreyfus, was wrongfully convicted of spying for Germany. Subsequently France was deeply divided over 'the Affair', but the Republic emerged from the crisis with honour when Dreyfus was rehabilitated.

Tsar: Russian for 'Emperor'. The Tsar was an *autocrat* or absolute ruler.

Kaiser: German for 'Emperor'. Kaiser and Tsar are German and Russian versions of the imperial Roman 'Caesar'.

A later generation was able to rename it the First World War.

By an extraordinary chance, the young Adolf Hitler is clearly visible in this Munich crowd joyfully celebrating the outbreak of the First World War in August 1914.

Four years of war on this scale wrecked the old European order and destroyed four great empires. The first to go was Russia, where the Tsar was overthrown in February 1917. The subsequent October Revolution led to the remodelling of Russia into the Soviet Union (the USSR), a state controlled by the Bolshevik or Communist Party, organized as a socialist economy, and regarded as the champion of world revolution. The other great powers on both sides were deeply hostile to the new state, and after the failure of their efforts to overthrow it they continued to treat it with the utmost suspicion. The fact that the USSR was a virtual outcast from the international community would have far-reaching consequences during the 1930s.

For example, the failure of Britain, France and the USSR to reach agreement even in 1939 (see page 15).

The other empires fell just before the end of the Great War. In 1917 the United States joined the Entente, and the Germans failed in their last desperate effort to win before the Americans arrived in force. In 1918, with her armies in retreat and a naval blockade starving out the home front, the German Empire collapsed and was replaced by a democratic republic, known from the city where it was formally established as the Weimar Republic. Almost simultaneously Austria-Hungary fell to pieces and the Habsburgs were unseated. A similar fate befell the Turkish Empire.

The victorious powers imposed a series of treaties and other arrangements – known for convenience as 'the Versailles settlement' – that transformed the map of Europe. The German government was forced to admit Germany's 'war-guilt' and, among other punishments, was condemned to lose a number of territories, accept the occupation of the Saar and Rhineland, limit Germany's armed forces, and to pay huge 'reparations' over a period of years to the victors. Rightly or wrongly, Germans felt that they had been unjustly penalized and humiliated by the Versailles settlement, and in the years to come this grievance would be exploited for all it was worth by Hitler and the Nazis.

It was at Versailles that the most important of the treaties between the Entente powers and Germany was signed.

Reparations: a war indemnity, or 'damages'.

The collapse of the Russian and Austrian empires led to the creation of

Representatives of the victorious Allies pose outside the railway carriage in which the armistice of 1918 was signed. In 1940 Hitler vengefully staged the same scene for the representatives of defeated France.

Free City: an independent city, not part of a state. For the League of Nations, see the paragraph on page 11.

Ethnic problems persist to this day in the region. Can you identify some of them?

Sudeten Germans: The Sudetenland was a highly industrialized region of Czechoslovakia whose population was mainly German.

a new group of East European nation states. An independent Poland was resurrected from the territories partitioned over a century earlier by Russia, Prussia and Austria. And so that the new state should have an outlet to the sea, she was given a 'Polish Corridor' – a broad strip of territory running through Germany to the Baltic Sea, even though this involved separating one part of Germany (East Prussia) from the rest of the country. The Corridor was served by the Baltic port of Danzig, which was taken from Germany and declared a Free City administered by the League of Nations.

Three new states, Austria, Hungary and Czechoslovakia, replaced the Habsburg empire, whose southernmost provinces were united with Serbia and Montenegro to form another newcomer, Yugoslavia. The intention was to stabilize the region by dividing it into single-nation states; but this was achieved to only a limited extent. Here too, the arrangements tended to penalize the Germans, among other things forbidding any union between the Weimar Republic and Austria, which in its new form was overwhelmingly German. And in any case the whole of Eastern Europe was (and is) an impossibly complicated ethnic patchwork; there was simply no way in which the map could have been drawn to create viable national states without the presence of substantial minorities inside their boundaries. Many such minorities existed, notably the three million strong population of Sudeten Germans who lived in the border areas of Czechoslovakia. This area had never been part of Germany, so the Versailles settlement could hardly have been expected to hand it over to a defeated and 'war-guilty' Reich; but an even more important consideration was the strategic value of this mountainous area, without which Czechoslovakia would be helpless against an attack from Germany.

The 1920s

German grievances and the situation in Eastern Europe were potentially –

The League of Nations was the direct 'ancestor' of the present United Nations Organization.

but only potentially – dangerous; given a long period of peace and prosperity, past antagonisms might have faded away. It was in the hope of settling international disputes peacefully that a League of Nations was set up in 1919.

In Central and Eastern Europe the early post-war years were troubled and confused. But, surprisingly, the most ominous developments took place in Italy – one of the victor-states of 1918 – where political and economic weakness led to the overthrow of the parliamentary system. Power was seized in 1922 by Benito Mussolini and his Fascist movement, whose unapologetic brutality and self-proclaimed contempt for democratic and humanitarian values had not been seen before in a supposedly civilized country. As a doctrine, Fascism was ferociously anti-Communist, made a cult of leadership, and extolled instinct, strength and action. There were many points of sympathy between Fascism and Nazism, and Hitler introduced a number of Fascist practices, such as the outstretched-arm Roman salute, into his own movement. Confusingly, 'fascism' is often used as a general term to describe Italian Fascism, Nazism and similar movements characterized by a one-party dictatorship, the militarization of society and totalitarian organization.

Totalitarian: word applied to states where virtually every aspect of life (not just politics) is affected by the controlling ideology.

In Germany a major crisis developed in 1923, when a failure to keep up reparations payments led to the occupation of Germany's great industrial district, the Ruhr, by French troops. German attempts at passive resistance led to the disruption of an already weakened economy; and that triggered a massive inflation in which paper currency became almost worthless, wiping out most people's personal savings. A large section of the middle class was impoverished, adding to the list of potentially explosive German resentments. However, the immediate crisis was overcome, although not before one attempt had been made to overthrow the Weimar Republic. Adolf Hitler, now the leader of a small nationalist party, the Nazis, tried to seize power by force in Munich, capital of the large southern province of Bavaria; but this 'Beer Hall Putsch' was easily quelled, and Hitler was sent to prison for a time.

Putsch: German term for a rising or revolt.

The fascist hero-cult, personified by the Italian dictator, Benito Mussolini.

National and international stability seemed to be in sight by the mid-1920s. The 1924 Dawes Plan helped Germany to meet her reparations payments, which were eventually lightened by being rescheduled to cover a longer period. In 1925 the French withdrew from the Ruhr and the Locarno treaties improved relations between the former belligerents. And by the late 1920s the German economy, rebuilt with loans from the United States, was in an apparently flourishing condition.

Hitler takes power

Then disaster struck. In 1929 the collapse of share prices on Wall Street triggered a depression which spread from the United States to the rest of the world, damaging the economies of all the industrialized nations. Germany – dependent on loans that were now being called in – was particularly hard hit. With banks and factories closing, unemployment soared (it eventually reached at least six millions) and German society was again shaken to its foundations.

One result was to increase support among Germans for political parties that offered radical cures for their afflictions. In the general election of September 1930 the Nazis scored an extraordinary success, emerging from near-obscurity to become the second largest party in the country. Over the following eighteen months the Nazis made steady progress, and by July 1932 they were polling far more votes than their closest rivals. But they were still far short of an absolute majority in the Reichstag. Other parties – including the Nationalists, the Catholic Centre, the Social Democrats and the Communists – were too hostile to one another to form a coalition government, so Germany remained in a state of political crisis in the early 1930s as one election followed another with no conclusive outcome in sight.

Meanwhile, a series of conservative-minded chancellors governed as best they could through emergency decrees issued by the President, Paul von Hindenburg, whose age and military reputation commanded a certain respect from most Germans. But this meant that backstage intrigues, not parliamentary support, determined who should be chancellor of Germany; and eventually Hindenburg was persuaded to appoint Hitler as chancellor on 30 January 1933.

The Nazis were soon able to make themselves undisputed masters of Germany, and within an astonishingly short time, all democratic institutions had disappeared. The Weimar Republic ceased to exist, and a new, one-party totalitarian state was born: the Third Reich.

'Wall Street': the New York stock-exchange. The collapse was 'The Wall Street Crash'.

The wider impact of the Depression, and the links between economic collapse and the rise of Nazism, are examined in Nathaniel Harris, *The Great Depression*, Batsford, 1988.

Reichstag: Germany's parliament.

Hindenburg was Chief of the German General Staff during the First World War.

Chancellor: prime minister of Germany.

'Reich' is usually translated as 'empire' or 'realm', although neither of these is completely satisfactory. From the Nazi point of view the first Reich was the medieval Holy Roman Empire (Heilige Römisches Reich); the second was the German Empire ruled by the Kaisers (1871-1918) and so Hitler's Germany was the Third Reich. Evidently the Weimar Republic ('anti-national', run by Jews etc.) did not count! What we call 'Austria' is properly Österreich, the Eastern Realm.

Berlin in 1929: stormtroopers march. With the Depression, the Nazis began to attract millions of voters.

Chancellor Adolf Hitler addresses the Nazi party faithful.

Sir Oswald Mosley's British Union of Fascists achieved much notoriety but never gained a mass following.

The road to war

During the 1930s Hitler was increasingly acclaimed as a god-like figure by the Germans, and Germany presented a united face to the world. A vigilant secret police and concentration camps ensured that all dissent was stifled; but also it seems likely that the regime was genuinely popular. Nazi spending on public works and rearmament pulled Germany out of the Depression and created jobs; Hitler's foreign policy triumphs boosted German pride; and a relentless, unchallenged propaganda imprinted these achievements on the minds of a captive audience.

Some observers during the 1930s began to predict that the age of democracy was over, as not only Germany but other fascist states registered one success after another. In 1935 Mussolini extended Italy's colonial empire by initiating the conquest of Abyssinia (Ethiopia). In 1936 Hitler sent troops into the Rhineland, German territory that had been demilitarized as part of the Versailles settlement. During the Spanish Civil War (1936-9) Italy and Germany despatched 'volunteer' forces to ensure the victory of General Franco's Fascist armies; Britain and France followed a policy of 'non-intervention' that meant leaving the Spanish Republic to its doom. By this time Germany and Italy were tending to work together, their partnership becoming known as the Axis, and more or less influential fascist parties had been established in most European countries including Britain. And in the Far East imperial Japan became an increasingly militarized, semi-fascist society, which in 1937 followed up earlier aggressions against China with an all-out invasion. The League of Nations

Europe in 1938

This was another breach of the Versailles settlement

The four powers were Germany, Italy, Britain and France; the exclusion of the USSR emphasized her isolation and probably helped to convince the Soviet leader Stalin that he must find allies where he could.

failed to control any of these developments, and hopes for a new international order faded away.

The march of events became even faster in 1938, when Hitler proclaimed the Anschluss – the union of Germany and Austria – and proceeded almost immediately to demand the return of Czechoslovakia's Sudeten Germans to the Reich. The governments of Britain and France were committed to a policy of 'appeasement' – that is, of placating Hitler by making concessions. They hoped to avoid another World War, and they felt that German grievances did have a certain justification. Moreover, they were quite glad to see a strong anti-Communist Germany making Central Europe safe from revolution or Soviet expansion. They therefore rejected Soviet offers of co-operation against Hitler, and in September 1938 a four-power conference at Munich arranged for vital areas of Czechoslovakia to be handed over to Germany. The British Prime Minister, Neville Chamberlain, believed that he brought back from Munich 'peace in our time'; and in 1938 many British and French people agreed with him, although many subsequent commentators have condemned the appeasers as short-sighted.

In the spring of 1939, having encouraged further unrest in Czechoslovakia, Hitler established a protectorate over most of the country

German troops, smiling for the camera, break down frontier barriers as the invasion of Poland begins.

A protectorate is a territory controlled but not annexed by a more powerful state, whose 'protective' role is supposedly benevolent. In the case of Bohemia and Moravia, the setting up of protectorates – rather than absorbing them into the Reich – was designed to make German actions seem less blatantly aggressive.

For the nature of the Nazi-Soviet pact, see text and marginal note on page 50.

(the Protectorate of Bohemia and Moravia). Mussolini, now very much the junior partner in the Axis, annexed Albania, and a formal German-Italian alliance, the 'Pact of Steel', was signed in May 1939. Since Bohemia and Moravia were emphatically not territories inhabited by Germans, Hitler's excuses seemed less convincing than before, and British and French attitudes began to harden. When it became clear that Poland was the next German target, Britain and France pledged themselves to come to her assistance if she was attacked, but failed to clinch an alliance with the USSR; instead, it was the Germans who came to terms, concluding a non-aggression pact with the Soviet Union in August 1939. When this was followed by a German invasion of Poland, the British and French governments honoured their pledges and declared war on 3 September 1939. As is well known, the European war eventually became a World War that ended in 1945 with the utter defeat of Nazi Germany, Fascist Italy and imperial Japan.

The defeats begin: Germans dead in the Russian snow.

Interpretations

The Formative Years

The young Hitler

Adolf Hitler was born on 20 April 1889 at Braunau in Austria-Hungary, where his father, Alois Hitler, was a customs official. The Hitlers moved from Braunau a few months after Adolf's birth, and in 1895, when Alois retired, they went to live just outside the provincial town of Linz in Upper Austria. This was where Hitler went to school and grew up.

Alois Hitler was almost 50 when he married his third wife, Klara Pölzl, a relation who was over 20 years younger. Of Klara's five children, only Adolf and his sister Paula survived infancy. It seems likely that maternal anxiety caused Klara to spoil her son, whereas the ageing ex-official remained a remote, forbidding and possibly punitive figure. Such evidence as exists certainly indicates that Hitler disliked his father and adored his mother.

Attempts to 'explain' Hitler in terms of his family life do not carry much conviction, but his school record is revealing. He did well at the primary

Braunau was on the border between Germany and Austria; characteristically, Hitler was to claim that there was a providential quality about his birth on this spot, between the two great Germanic lands that he was destined to unite.

This is also true of Alois Hitler's illegitimacy, and of the possibility (no more than that) that his unknown father was Jewish.

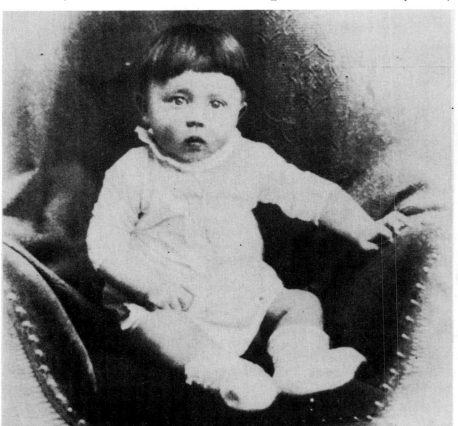

Baby Adolf.

level, but then failed consistently at the two secondary schools he attended. His teachers' reports indicated that he was not without ability, but would not apply himself and resented correction. He left school at sixteen without having gained the certificate required for higher educational purposes.

After Alois's death in 1903 Klara moved with Adolf to Linz, where her pension supported them while he spent the years 1905-7 dreaming about becoming a great artist, going to the opera (where he acquired his lifelong passion for the music-dramas of Richard Wagner), and wandering about the town with his admiring friend August Kubizek. It already seemed possible that he would become a ne'er-do-well.

However, in the autumn of 1907 he did move to Vienna, hoping to secure admission to the Academy of Fine Arts. In October 1907, and again the following year, Hitler submitted examples of his work, and was rejected. According to his own account, this 'bolt from the blue' was made bearable only because he was advised that his talents lay not in painting but in architecture, which he henceforth regarded as his vocation. He clung to this conviction, although he seems never to have taken any practical steps towards becoming an architect. Instead he experienced in Vienna 'five

Richard Wagner (1813-83). His *Ring of the Nibelung* evokes the gods and heroes of Germanic myth; its vision of the world became part of the Nazi ethos – and all the more influential because, coincidentally or not, Wagner was an ardent anti-semite.

Hitler at sixteen, sketched by a fellow-pupil. At this time his chosen image was evidently that of a bohemian artist.

Watercolour by the young Hitler. His paintings are certainly conventional, but perhaps not so contemptible as is often made out.

These and later quotations are taken from Hitler's book *Mein Kampf,* which contains much (not very trustworthy) autobiographical material. It is more fully discussed on pages 27-30.

Some of Hitler's Viennese acquaintances deny this, so it is possible that *Mein Kampf* exaggerates Hitler's political development in order to make his years in Vienna seem more usefully occupied than they actually were.

Conscription: compulsory military service.

Imperial Germany was a young state, united only in 1871 under the King of Prussia, who became Kaiser or Emperor. The rulers of other German states, including the King of Bavaria, kept their titles and a degree of independence. Even after 1918 Bavarian monarchism and separatism influenced German politics – and Hitler's career.

This was of course true of millions of people in both World Wars. Does it tell us anything about the nature and quality of modern life?

years of hardship and misery' while he 'studied as never before'. First as a day labourer, later as an artist in a small way, he earned 'a truly meagre living which never sufficed to appease even my daily hunger'.

Actually Hitler's inheritances from his parents, plus the orphan's pension he received from the state and the handouts sent by an aunt, should have given him a reasonable income even when spread over a five-year period. Nevertheless there is evidence to suggest that he slept rough during the summer of 1909, and records prove that from autumn 1909 until May 1913 he lived in Viennese men's hostels. This certainly presented a loss of social status, although the lack of responsibility and loose-knit relationships inherent in the hostel may well have suited Hitler. He earned some money by painting postcard pictures which a partner sold for him, and by designing posters for local firms. When in funds he spent hours in cafés reading newspapers or declaiming at temporary companions, although he could not bear to be contradicted. It is generally believed that he was already a passionate nationalist and anti-semite; and although he struck some people as oddly impressive, he also appeared increasingly eccentric – a strange, essentially solitary man, shut up in a world of fantasies.

Nevertheless, Hitler was not entirely fixed in his habits. In May 1913 he suddenly left Austria-Hungary and settled at Munich, the capital of Bavaria. One motive may have been a wish to avoid conscription, which would have placed him cheek by jowl with Austria's 'promiscuous swarm of foreign peoples' and made him the defender of a cosmopolitan state he detested. In fact Hitler had already failed to register for military service two years running in Vienna. However, the Austrian authorities caught up with him in Munich, and in February 1914 he returned to Vienna to take his medical examination – and was pronounced unfit for service.

Ironically, the First World War broke out only six months after Hitler's return to Bavaria. By an extraordinary chance, a photograph survives of Bavarians hearing the news, and Hitler's face is visible in the cheering crowd. But in any case his patriotic emotion is beyond doubt, since he immediately petitioned the King of Bavaria for permission to serve in the army. It was granted, and he joined up as a private in the Sixteenth Bavarian Reserve Infantry Regiment.

As a German, Hitler welcomed the war. But it also had a personal significance for him, since

it offered the opportunity to slough off the frustration, failure, and resentment of the last six years. Here was an escape from the tension and dissatisfaction of a lonely individuality into the excitement and warmth of a close, disciplined, collective life, in which he could identify himself with the power and purpose of a great organization.

Alan Bullock, *Hitler: a study in tyranny,* Pelican, 1962.

As this suggests, the war ended an entire phase of Hitler's life, setting him on a new path.

Discovering a vocation

Hitler was a good soldier. He served all through the four years of the war, was wounded in 1916, and was gassed and temporarily blinded in the final weeks of the conflict. As early as December 1914 he was awarded the Iron Cross, Second Class, and just before the end, in August 1918, he received the Iron Cross, First Class – a decoration rarely bestowed on a corporal. In view of this, it is curious that Hitler never became an officer, and ironic that his superiors put a low estimate on the leadership potential of their future

Commander-in-Chief! Evidently Hitler still gave an impression of eccentricity; by the standards of ordinary soldiers he was so wrapped up in his duty and the fatherland – and so notably lacking in a normal private life – that he seemed to be something of a freak. Later, when he found the right setting and was seen from below, he would be admired for his dedication: when it comes to reputations, the angle of vision is everything.

Do you agree?

With some justification, Hitler believed that the rigidly disciplined German army was the best in the world, and so his war experiences confirmed his faith in Germanic superiority and the virtues of authority and obedience. This made defeat all the harder to bear, especially when it came with staggering suddenness. German reverses in the field had been concealed from the public until the last moment, and Hitler himself was in hospital after being gassed when a padre announced that revolution had broken out, the Kaiser had abdicated, and Germany had lost the war.

One result of this concealment was that it became easy to believe in the myth of 'Germany's unbeaten armies', described in the marginal note on page 28.

Again everything went black before my eyes; I tottered and groped my way back to the dormitory, threw myself on my bunk, and dug my burning head into my blankets and pillow.

Since the day when I had stood at my mother's grave, I had not wept. When in my youth Fate seized me with merciless hardness, my defiance mounted. When in the long war years Death snatched so many a dear comrade and friend from our ranks, it would have seemed to me almost a sin to complain – after all, were they not dying for Germany? . . . But now I could not help it. Only now did I see how all personal suffering vanishes in comparison with the misfortunes of the fatherland.

Hitler, *Mein Kampf.*

Apart from his distress at Germany's defeat, does this passage tell us anything about Hitler's personality and outlook?

Hitler as a soldier, with First World War comrades.

Another questionable autobiographical statement from *Mein Kampf*.

Soviet republic: state run by workers' and soldiers' councils, on the lines of the state set up by the Bolsheviks in Russia (see page 9).

As a result of this shock – and of his anger at the supposed betrayal of Germany – 'I, for my part, decided to go into politics.' If so, he did very little about it for some time. Still attached to the army, he returned to Munich and lived obscurely in barracks while post-war Germany was swept with disorders until the Weimar government managed to regain control; we do not even know what part Hitler played in the short-lived soviet republic which was set up in Munich before being ferociously suppressed in March 1919. Perhaps he was still drifting, 'keeping a low profile', waiting for events to give him a push in a definite direction. This certainly fits what we know about the young Hitler – drawing up grandiose designs while waiting for providence to make him a famous architect.

Providence duly obliged in mid-1919, when an officer, realizing that sections of the army were still influenced by leftist sentiments, set up courses to train political agents who would indoctrinate the troops with 'national' opinions. Hitler was among those chosen, and he proved a brilliant success. This was probably the point at which he became aware of his gifts as a speaker and propagandist. He was entrusted with a variety of missions, including confidential assignments such as reporting on the numerous political groups that were active in Bavaria.

One such group was the German Workers' Party, founded in January 1919. Hitler visited it eight months later and – with the approval of his superiors – decided to join. Even in his uncandid autobiography, *Mein Kampf*, it is clear that he was attracted to the party because of the scope it offered to his talents. It was based on the sort of nationalist, anti-semitic and anti-Bolshevik views that Hitler also held, but there were a good many such groups in Munich. More important, it was small and ineffective:

aside from a few directives, there was nothing, no programme, no leaflet, no printed matter at all, no membership cards, not even a miserable rubber stamp, only obvious good faith and good intentions.
Hitler, *Mein Kampf.*

This 'dull organization' (as Hitler called it) was ripe to be taken over by an ambitious individual with political insight. That is one way of putting it. Hitler said much the same thing, but in words that make his decision to join the party sound far less self-serving:

What assumptions underlie this way of describing Hitler's motives, by contrast with the version from *Mein Kampf* that follows?

This absurd little organization with its few members seemed to me to possess the one advantage that it had not frozen into an 'organization', but left the individual an opportunity for real personal activity. Here it was still possible to work, and the smaller the movement, the more readily it could be put into the proper form. Here the content, the goal, and the road could still be determined, which in the existing great parties was impossible from the outset.
Hitler, *Mein Kampf.*

The membership cards of the German Workers' Party were numbered in conventional fashion – except that they began at No. 501, presumably in order to conceal how few they were. So when Adolf Hitler joined the party, he became member number 555.

The Politician

The Putsch: forced march or Hitler's folly?

Hitler entered the German Workers' Party as member No. 7 of its executive committee; characteristically he would later allow it to be believed that he was the seventh member of the party itself. He was given responsibility for propaganda and recruitment, and immediately began to show his mettle. Within a few months the party was attracting public attention through posters, press notices and meetings. Then it acquired its own newspaper, the *Völkische Beobachter*, and a new name: the Nazionalsozialistische Deutsche Arbeiterpartei (National Socialist German Workers' Party or NSDAP), soon familiarly abbreviated to Nazi Party. The swastika symbol was taken over from an Austrian nationalist group and incorporated in a new party flag, while the Italian Fascists – currently making headlines – provided the outstretched-arm Roman salute. Ex-servicemen swelled the numbers of the new movement and provided recruits for its paramilitary arm, the SA (*Sturmabteilung* or Stormtroop), established in August 1921. As well as its characteristic institutions and symbols, the Nazi Party also acquired many of its leading figures in Munich during this period, notably the tough ex-fighter pilot ace Hermann Göring, Rudolf Hess, Alfred Rosenberg and Ernst Röhm, a scar-faced regular soldier through whom Hitler could maintain valuable contacts with the army in Bavaria.

Paramilitary: describes a civilian group or organization which is structured on military lines and, usually, equipped with some kind of uniform or distinguishing marks.

Hitler himself left the army in April 1920 to devote all his energies to party work. The meteoric rise of the Nazis from an obscure club to a position of influence in Bavarian politics was essentially his achievement as organizer, propagandist and speaker – and the fact was realized when an internal crisis developed in July 1921. Angered by approaches made to other nationalist groups while he was away in Berlin, Hitler resigned from the party, stating that he would reconsider only if he was granted dictatorial powers – the kind of demand that in most instances positively invites rejection. Yet the party executive agreed. Their reply is a remarkable document, for it was written by men who knew him, and before his power and success commanded automatic deference and flattery. In other words, it is a sincere tribute:

The committee is prepared, in acknowledgement of your tremendous knowledge, your singular dedication and selfless service to the Movement, and your rare oratorical gift, to concede to you dictatorial powers, and will be most delighted if you will take over the position of First Chairman . . . .
Quoted in Joachim C. Fest, *Hitler*, Weidenfeld and Nicolson, 1974.

Fest believes that Hitler's absence in Berlin was partly a manoeuvre to provoke a crisis. By contrast, a more recent writer describes Hitler as resigning 'in a fit of pique', and quotes another historian (Tyrell) in support of his argument that Hitler was *not* aiming at personal supremacy:

What does a writer imply when he begins a sentence with the word 'True'?

True, as the price of his return to the fold, Hitler insisted on dictatorial powers to reconstruct the party. Tyrell maintains that this was basically a negative reaction on Hitler's part motivated solely by a wish to prevent the party moving in a direction of which he disapproved.
William Carr, *Hitler: A Study in Personality and Politics*, Arnold, 1978.

One objection to this line of argument is that the demand (for dictatorial powers) was out of all proportion to its supposed aim (to prevent the adoption of a certain kind of policy – an aim that could have been achieved with less risk by demanding a straightforward pledge from the executive). The most satisfactory explanation is surely the simple, common-sense one – that Hitler demanded dictatorial powers because he wanted unchallenged authority, either for its own sake or because he felt that he alone knew what was best for the party.

The Carr/Tyrell view minimizes Hitler's lust for power in support of a wider argument – that Hitler did not see himself from the first as the man chosen by 'Providence' to save Germany. By contrast, the long-established interpretation is that

> Then and there, in July 1921, was established the 'leadership principle' which was to be the law first of the Nazi Party and then of the Third Reich. 'The Führer' had arrived on the German scene.
> William L. Shirer, *The Rise and Fall of the Third Reich*, Secker, 1960.

More recent writings have emphasized statements by Hitler in which he claimed to be the 'drummer' of the 'national revolution', preparing the way for some greater man, yet to appear, who would consummate it; he occasionally spoke in this vein even in the mid-1920s, although by that time the 'Führer cult' was going strong. This certainly makes Hitler a more credible, 'ordinary' figure, coping with a fluctuating self-image that only became fixed when events gave it final definition. Until the mid-to-late 1920s he must have borne in mind the possibility that a powerful nationalist party might develop in north Germany before the Bavarian-based Nazis made any impact there – in which case he would inevitably become the junior partner in any subsequent 'national revolution'.

However, the possibility that he might play a secondary, 'drummer' role does not necessarily mean that Hitler saw himself as a propagandist rather than a leader. The Number Two in a national revolution is also a leader. Power can be exercised at many levels, and there is plenty of evidence that Hitler wanted as much of it as he could get. He may not yet have been certain that he was to be the infallible Führer of the German people, but he certainly intended to rule within his party, and to make the party as influential as he could.

Luckily for Hitler, the situation in Bavaria was extremely favourable. Many right-wing, nationalist, military and monarchist groups hated the Weimar Republic, and in 1920 a serious attempt was made to overthrow it. The Kapp Putsch failed in Berlin, but its equivalent succeeded in Bavaria. From this time onwards, Bavaria was ruled by extreme right-wing governments, backed by a sympathetic local army command. Bavaria did not come out in open rebellion against the hated national government in Berlin, but it became a haven for Freikorps and other groups no longer tolerated elsewhere. Many of these swelled the SA, whose strong-arm tactics against Social Democrats and other opponents gave them control of the Munich streets – thanks to the sympathetic non-action of the authorities, who also looked favourably on the intensification of Nazi propaganda. By 1922 party membership was rising fast, and Nazism had begun to make some converts even outside Bavaria.

Freikorps: Free Corps. Right-wing para-military groups, mainly ex-servicemen, who were active during the chaotic period following the defeat of Germany.

Nineteen twenty-three was a crisis year for the Weimar Republic and the young Nazi Party. The French occupied the Ruhr and the German government ordered a policy of passive resistance that caused economic disruption. Inflation, already alarmingly high, went completely out of control, so that paper currency became almost worthless. The Berlin government was challenged not only by the Bavarian Right but by the Left in other states. By September, when the government admitted defeat over the Ruhr by calling off the passive resistance campaign, the collapse of the Weimar Republic seemed to be a distinct possibility. In Bavaria a State of Emergency was declared and a triumvirate became the effective rulers of the province: state commissioner Gustav von Kahr, who nominally wielded dictatorial powers, chief of police Hans von Seisser, and General Otto von Lossow, who commanded the German armed forces in Bavaria. In view of the situation, it seemed highly likely that these men would either declare

Triumvirate: association of three people as rulers.

Bavarian independence or use the province as a springboard for an offensive against the hated Republic.

Hitler's plan to take advantage of the crisis is well described by William L. Shirer:

How could such a small party overthrow the Republic? Hitler, who was not easily discouraged by odds against him, thought he saw a way. He might unite under his leadership all the anti-republican, nationalist forces in Bavaria. Then with the support of the Bavarian government, the armed leagues and the Reichswehr stationed in Bavaria, he might lead a march on Berlin – as Mussolini had marched on Rome the year before – and bring the Weimar Republic down.
Shirer, *The Rise and Fall of the Third Reich*.

Reichswehr: German armed forces. Under Hitler the name was changed to Wehrmacht.

The reference to Mussolini's example is of crucial importance. The famous 'March on Rome' by the Fascists was not an attack but a kind of threatening mass demonstration; Mussolini himself went by train. Yet it was enough to bring down the government and persuade Italy's rulers to install Mussolini as prime minister, even though the Fascists were only a minority party. A demoralized parliamentary system and, among the ruling and propertied classes, fear of red revolution, enabled Mussolini to bluff his way to power without firing a shot.

Compare this with Hitler's attitude in 1932-33 (page 33).

This was the example that Hitler hoped to follow: he always intended to work with the state apparatus, not to fight against it. On May Day 1923 he even accepted a serious loss of prestige rather than risk a clash with army and police units; when they demanded the return of army weapons which the Nazis had 'borrowed' for an attack on the Bavarian Left, Hitler ordered his followers to hand them over. A 'national revolution' which began with fighting between two sets of 'national' forces could hardly hope to succeed.

In September the situation again became promising, and it seemed likely that the triumvirate would lead a march on Berlin. Hitler strengthened his position by becoming the leader of the Kampfbund, a coalition of radical right-wing groups, and also by associating himself with Erich Ludendorff, a legendary First World War military leader whose reputation was second only to Hindenburg's.

But although the triumvirate conferred with the Kampfbund and other rightist groups, the 'march' failed to materialize all through October and into November. Evidently Kahr and his associates were reluctant to commit themselves and risk facing charges of treason if they failed. They may well have believed that the army would do their work for them in Berlin; but instead the opposite occurred. The army stood by the Weimar government and suppressed the Right and Left impartially; and with currency reform heralding a possible return to normality, the chances of overthrowing the Republic began to fade.

Currency reform helped to restore confidence in the Mark, eventually stabilizing its value and ending the worst of the inflation.

Hitler resolved to make the triumvirs act before it was too late; he would use a degree of force to mobilize them – not to overthrow them – despite the events on May Day, which indicated that there were limits to army and police collusion with the nationalists. The putsch of 8-9 November 1923 can only be described briefly here; but its events are worth closer study, since they provide interesting insights into the role played in history by accident and improvisation. On the night of 8 November, Hitler's followers surrounded the Burgerbräukeller beer hall, where Kahr, Seisser and Lossow were speaking at a meeting. Hitler burst in, fired his pistol at the ceiling to command attention, and proclaimed the establishment of a new German government, with himself as president. Leading positions were to be given to the triumvirs – who were promptly arrested and shuffled into a side room. The hostility of the crowd melted away when Hitler announced

Hardly the position a 'drummer' would award himself? See page 22.

The Beer Hall putsch: stormtroopers on the move.

(falsely) that the triumvirs had agreed to join him; and then the enthusiasm of the crowd, audible in the side room, helped to persuade the triumvirs, who were also impressed by Ludendorff's backing for the putsch. By a successful double bluff Hitler seemed to have launched the 'national revolution' and to have placed himself at its head.

Then things went badly wrong. Hitler was called away, and in his absence Kahr, Seisser and Lossow were allowed to leave; Ludendorff approved, believing that as officers and gentlemen they could be trusted not to break their promises to Hitler and himself. But they did just that – not unreasonably, since the promises had been extorted at gunpoint. They denounced the putsch, proclaimed the NSDAP dissolved, and took control of the city.

When their defection became clear, Hitler fell into a state of despair, realizing that the basic assumption of the putsch – that the authorities would co-operate – had been completely falsified. Its most famous episode – the march on Munich the following day – actually represented a desperate final effort to save a lost cause. There was plenty of popular support for the putsch, and the Kampfbund leaders evidently believed it might still be possible to generate a wave of enthusiasm and win over the army and police. A column of several thousand men, with Hitler and Ludendorff at its head, marched into Munich until it was faced by a contingent of police that refused to let it pass.

As often happens in such circumstances, some unknown individual fired a bullet, and fighting started. In this instance the exchange of shots lasted only a few seconds. Hitler had linked arms with the man beside him, who was killed, pulling Hitler down and dislocating his shoulder. Sixteen putschists and three policemen were killed, and many more people were injured. Then the members of the column threw themselves on the ground or scattered. Only Ludendorff stayed upright and marched through the police cordon. He and other leading putschists were arrested; Hitler was taken into custody two days later at a friend's house.

The Beer Hall putsch: Nazis man the barricades. The bespectacled young man with the flag is Heinrich Himmler, later chief of the infamous SS.

Historians have criticized Hitler's behaviour on a number of counts. One eminent German writer dismisses the entire project as misconceived and mistimed:

The Hitler putsch was an epilogue, not a main event, in this incredibly confused and miserable story [the German crisis of 1923]. In November the young madman [Hitler] attempted what might have been successful a few months earlier. He thought that he could rouse his past supporters, officials, monarchists and leaders of the Bavarian Reichswehr division to action by putting a pistol to their heads. But they ran away as soon as they were no longer threatened by his pistol . . . Ludendorff and Hitler found themselves alone with a handful of personal supporters whom the police put down with one salvo.
Golo Mann, *The History of Germany Since 1789*, Chatto, 1968.

To what extent are descriptions of 'good' and 'bad' timing a matter of hindsight?

This scarcely takes into account the difficulties of Hitler's position, or tells us how or when he should have acted. After all, he *had* tried earlier, on May Day – or should we be equally wise after the event here and pronounce this attempt *too* early?

Other historians have pointed out that, having built up a rabid, action-hungry following, Hitler was virtually obliged to set it in motion. Shortly after the putsch, one SA commander claimed that

I myself told Hitler: one of these days I will not be able to hold the men back. Unless something happens now, the men will take off on you.
Wilhelm Brückner, quoted in Fest, *Hitler*.

Especially after the climb-down in May, Hitler could not remain inactive without losing all credit with his own followers. This is an interesting line of argument, since it reveals the extent to which even the most dictatorial or obsessive of leaders has to come to terms with his followers' expectations.

Many comments on Hitler's personal behaviour during the crisis are coloured by an unwillingness to grant him a single admirable quality. Much has been made of a witness who claimed that Hitler was literally the first to make a getaway after the clash with the police – although it is hard

Does the language used in this quotation tell us anything about its user's prejudices?

to know how he could be sure when men were scattering in all directions. Shirer is fairly typical in writing that Hitler 'had run away at the first hail of bullets', while Fest and many others compare him unfavourably with Ludendorff. On the other hand:

> One could just as easily argue that Ludendorff behaved in a foolhardy manner . . . . Cowardly Hitler was not, as his war record proves. But to stay behind with the smell of defeat in the air would have been a romantic gesture out of keeping with his sense of political realism.
> Carr, *Hitler*.

Moreover, Ludendorff was a venerable figure whom no German soldier or policeman would deliberately shoot: he could afford the romantic gesture where Hitler could not. A final point, somehow always overlooked, is that Hitler was in a good deal of pain from his shoulder and hardly fit to lead any cause, let alone a hopelessly lost one.

The putsch has often been described as a fiasco, but that was not how it was seen at the time in Munich. It was followed by several days of rioting in which Kahr, not Hitler, was jeered at and abused by Munichers. And when Hitler was brought to trial, he was treated, and presented himself, as quite the opposite of a ridiculous adventurer.

Hitler looks out on the world

In February 1924 Hitler and his fellow-conspirators were put on trial at the Munich infantry school. The proceedings were unusual, since the Bavarian establishment felt considerable sympathy with Hitler and allowed him to speechify as much as he pleased in the courtroom. The result was a triumph for the Nazi leader. Instead of trying to excuse himself, Hitler declared that the putsch had been completely justified, denounced the Berlin

Ludendorff (centre), Hitler and other defendants, on trial for their part in the Beer Hall putsch. Second from right is Ernst Röhm, later chief of Hitler's SA; Hitler had him shot after the 1934 purge.

government, and effectively put Kahr, Seisser and Lossow in the dock: these prosecution witnesses, supposedly the injured parties, found it hard to deny that they had contemplated (and discussed with Hitler) the very actions which were now being treated as crimes against the state. The Bavarian triumvirate emerged with tarnished reputations, while the accused, Adolf Hitler, appeared as a heroic, defiant figure who had launched a great patriotic venture.

In later years he was to go further, turning the anniversary of the putsch into a major commemorative event and elevating those who died to the rank of martyrs. One of Hitler's biographers comments on the raising of a memorial to them in 1935, when Hitler had been in power for two years:

Fair comment? These were the men whom twelve years before Hitler had left dying in the street while he fled. By skilful propaganda he had turned the fiasco of 1923 and his own failure as a leader into retrospective triumph.
Alan Bullock, *Hitler: a study in tyranny.*

In the event, Hitler received an extraordinarily light sentence – five years imprisonment, of which he served nine months after the trial before being released in November 1924. It was in the Landsberg prison, where he was comfortably lodged, that Hitler wrote *Mein Kampf*, the book which was to become the 'Bible' of the Nazi movement. It combines an unreliable account of Hitler's personal and political development with an all-too-clear account of his political ideas. It was not in fact written but dictated, mainly to Hitler's faithful follower Rudolf Hess. Although he had been persuaded that he should publish an autobiography while the public remained interested in the putsch, Hitler was impatient and scornful of the written word, for he believed that only speech moved the masses and so made history.

Why should platform and print require different approaches? *Mein Kampf* is not a great book. It is long-winded, repetitious and rhapsodic, in a style that is more effective on the platform than in print. Although it does have forceful passages (and is certainly not unreadable, as is sometimes implied), it lacks the qualities – including sustained argument – which might convert any reader not already inclined to racist-nationalist opinions. The ideas expressed are of extraordinary crudity, and are baldly asserted without any serious attempt to counter objections – again, the technique of the orator, not of the cooler, more critical medium of prose. Many of Hitler's statements fail to rise above the level of slovenly bar-room polemic and are obviously false – for example that the *entire* Viennese press was dominated by Jews, and that, when it came to the staff of the Social Democratic journals, 'from the publisher down, they were all Jews'.

But see page 44 for a dissenting view. Nevertheless Hitler's ideas are worth outlining because – more, perhaps, than most politicians – he made a determined effort to put them into practice when he achieved power. And, for all their crudity, they do form a system – that is, they are on the whole internally consistent, even if it is the consistency more commonly found in science fantasy than in political philosophy.

The supreme importance of race is Hitler's central belief. Every creative achievement, he insists, has been accomplished by the Aryan peoples, by which he seems to mean Europeans (though not Slavs), especially if they are of the blonde, blue-eyed 'racial' type. Other peoples can attain a certain level of culture if they are dominated by an Aryan minority, but relapse when – as happens sooner or later – the Aryans dilute their blood by inter-marrying with the 'lower human beings' whom they rule – something that Hitler fully intended to prevent when the Germans became conquerors and masters. The obsessive quality of Hitler's concern with racial purity, springing from some personal neurosis, is apparent everywhere in his writing. For example:

The lost purity of the blood alone destroys inner happiness forever, plunges men into the abyss for all time, and the consequences can never more be eliminated from body and spirit.
Mein Kampf

Here Hitler is contrasting 'the lost purity of the blood' with extremely severe misfortunes such as defeat in war, from which it is nonetheless possible to recover.

Hitler seems to have regarded the Germans as the purest Aryans. But if so, why had they lost the war, and why were so many Germans betraying the racial 'ideal' by supporting socialist and internationalist forces? Hitler found the answer in another racial factor: the Jews. Stateless, parasitic, uncreative, yet diabolically cunning, the Jews worked to undermine and pollute the blood of the Germans. This was the hidden cause of everything that had gone wrong, of everything Hitler had hated. Jews had weakened Germany even before the war had begun. They were capitalist exploiters who made the workers disaffected. They were also the Marxists who duped the same workers into turning against their fatherland. They were behind the 'November criminals' who had betrayed Germany's unbeaten armies, set up the hated Weimar Republic, and signed the shameful Versailles settlement. And they also controlled the press, were responsible for modernism in the arts ('literary filth, artistic trash and theatrical idiocy') and organized prostitution!

Marxists: followers of the socialist thinker Karl Marx. Modern Communist states claim to be based on his doctrines.

'Germany's unbeaten armies'. Many Germans preferred to believe that the army had been 'stabbed in the back' by treachery on the home front. The founders of the Weimar Republic were blamed for making a humiliating peace – despite the underpublicized fact that they had done so on the advice of the army leaders.

This was an extreme example of a 'scapegoat' theory – one that explains and excuses everything by putting the blame on an unpopular outsider. It was also an extreme example of a conspiracy theory, which presupposes the widespread, co-ordinated operation of secret powers as a moving force in history. In Hitler's version, the Jews pretend to be a religious group to conceal their racial otherness; Jewish capitalists, red revolutionaries and pimps act in concert to achieve the same ends; and their most potent invention – Marxism – purports to be about the redistribution of wealth but is actually designed to bring about economic chaos.

Historians tend to be sceptical about conspiracy theories. Can you think of some reasons why they should be?

As we have seen, Hitler's convictions about race were not just a matter of ideas, but sprang from some personal fixation that is revealed by the vocabulary of *Mein Kampf*. This is at its most violent and strange when the subject is the Jews:

With satanic joy in his face, the black-haired Jewish youth lurks in wait for the unsuspecting girl whom he defiles with his blood, thus stealing her from her people.
Mein Kampf.

Hitler's language implies some more violent solution than mere exclusion from the national life. Here the most moderate interpretation has been put on his words to avoid prejudging the issue raised on page 56.

Hitler uses 'culture' in the biological sense (a nourishing medium in which, e.g., a bacillus can be grown).

The practical consequences of these beliefs are spelled out in *Mein Kampf*. The Weimar Republic must be overthrown, the 'November criminals' punished and the Jews excluded from national life. Democracy and parliamentarianism must go: democracy 'is the forerunner of Marxism which without it would be unthinkable. It provides the world plague with the culture in which its germs can spread.' It also promotes mediocrities – crowd-pleasers and compromisers who never take hard or unpopular decisions. Instead, Germany must have a leader who will take responsibility for his actions – an obvious echo of Hitler's way of presenting himself in the Munich courtroom. Strongly led, Germany will repudiate the Versailles settlement, reassert control over all the national territories, and bring all Germans together in a single Reich.

Most historians have been impressed by the fact that this is just what Hitler did after he took power. And for this reason they have emphasized the significance of his longer-term aims, which can be related to his conduct of the Second World War. According to Hitler, the boundaries of the Reich were too narrow: the Germans needed *Lebensraum* (living-space), vast new areas in which to settle.

And so we National Socialists consciously draw a line beneath the foreign policy tendency of our pre-war period. We take up where we broke off six hundred years ago. We stop the endless German movement to the south and west, and turn our gaze towards the land in the east . . . and shift to the soil policy of the future . . . . If we speak of soil in Europe today, we can primarily have in mind only Russia *and her vassal border states.*
Mein Kampf

Italicized by Hitler in order to emphasize its fundamental importance in his thought.

A striking aspect of this view is that it regards the 'traditional' rivalry between Germany and France as of secondary importance. Yes, accounts will have to be settled with France, but this will 'achieve meaning only if it offers the rear cover for an enlargement of our people's living space in Europe'. Germany's destiny lay eastwards, in the territories inhabited by inferior Slavs and ruled by Jewish Bolsheviks!

The rivalry was traditional in the sense that France had for centuries tried to expand eastwards (most dramatically under Napoleon), and that the roles were then reversed when the new German Empire fought France in 1870-71 and again in 1914-18.

With such a philosophy, it is not surprising that Hitler had no use for attempts to limit war and conquest, for example through the League of Nations. On the contrary: he interpreted the history of the world as a series of ruthless struggles between states and races, in which no quarter was given and the fittest survived; and he claimed that this was a desirable outcome, since it eliminated weak and unhealthy peoples. Such a view was essentially based on Charles Darwin's theory of biological evolution by natural selection: when adapted to history and politics this is known as Social Darwinism; and, although it does not fit the facts of human history very well, it was fashionable in some quarters around 1900. Hitler did not originate it: he merely took it seriously.

Can you think of some objections to Social Darwinism? For example, is it really the 'unfit' who perish in wars?

Finally there is the question of the 'Socialism' in National Socialism. Most historians have been sceptical about Hitler's commitment to social justice, despite the condemnations of poverty and exploitation that abound in *Mein Kampf*. This is understandable, since in the twenties and thirties

Adolf Hitler on his release from prison, facing an apparently unpromising future.

Hitler constantly held back the more vocally anti-capitalist wing of the party; and when he came to power the workers gained jobs but lost most of their rights.

What is true is that Hitler was anti-bourgeois. He hated the respectable world which had rejected him, and despised its timidity and subservience to convention. But although he claimed that he wanted to abolish social classes, he intended to replace them with a new hierarchy – one in which most Germans would have a lowly place, but in which they would be compensated by becoming masters of inferior peoples. This is shown by a final quotation – one of many which could also be cited as evidence that *Mein Kampf* was not a youthful indiscretion, but represented the enduring 'granite foundation' of his political outlook. According to a refugee from Nazi Germany, Hitler told party officials in 1932 that in the future

Herren: masters.

There will be a *Herren*-class, a historical class tempered by battle, and welded from the most varied elements. There will be a great hierarchy of party members. They will be the new middle class. And there will be the great mass of the anonymous, the serving collective, the eternally disfranchised, no matter whether they were once members of the old bourgeoisie, the big landowning class, the working class or the artisans. Nor will their financial or previous social position be of the slightest importance. These preposterous differences will have been liquidated in a single revolutionary process. But beneath them there will still be the class of subject alien races; we need not hesitate to call them the modern slave class. And over all these will stand the new high aristocracy, the most deserving and the most responsible Führer personalities.
Hermann Rauschning, *Hitler Speaks*, 1939; quoted by Carr, *Hitler*.

Attaining power: luck or judgement?

During his imprisonment Hitler made no serious effort to hold together the National Socialist movement or the Kampfbund, both of which had officially been dissolved. In fact, by delegating authority to the politically incompetent race-theorist Alfred Rosenberg he almost certainly intended to ensure that no rival leader emerged, and that the future prospects of the movement seemed non-existent without him at its head.

Like many of Hitler's later tactics, this has rightly been seen as evidence of his all-pervading egoism. A more dubious conclusion from this episode is that, if Hitler was prepared to see the movement decline rather than risk his supremacy, his political convictions cannot have been sincerely held: that he was fundamentally a cynic or nihilist, using ideas as a means to acquire power for its own sake. This is surely an over-simple view of human psychology. Many politicians have managed to be at one and the same time self-serving and committed to a cause; and the messiah-type has the further advantage of believing that since he (or she) is the indispensable or chosen one, it would be a disaster if the cause were to be led by anyone else. So any expedient is justified if it prevents such a catastrophic development. Better than most people, messiahs are able to help out their idealism with large doses of self-interest.

Can you think of any examples – if possible from among Hitler's contemporaries in the western democracies?

Shortly after Hitler's release from prison, the ban on the Nazi Party was lifted. The movement was effectively re-founded in February 1925, with Hitler again installed as its unchallenged leader. Over the next few years his hold became even tighter, as propaganda and ritual generated a Führer-cult and Nazism became fully committed to the 'Führer principle' – that leaders should exercise unquestioned authority at every level of the party (and, later, of the state). This was a logical result of the NSDAP's military style, and of the Nazi rejection of parliamentarian and democratic principles. But it also, of course, suited Hitler, who emphasized his lonely

The Führer principle – making an idol of a single individual – also helped to disguise the internal contradictions of Nazism.

eminence by refusing to co-operate with any other nationalist group and breaking with former allies such as Ludendorff and Röhm.

Hitler's go-it-alone policy is sometimes characterized as another example of his egomania, which made him prefer to be the dominant figure in a small party rather than risk his position for the sake of the cause. No doubt the egomania existed; but it can also be argued that in this case Hitler's policy was shrewd and consistent. He made alliances when there seemed a chance of seizing power (in 1923, and again in the early 1930s). When there was no chance he emphasized the singleness of purpose and ideological purity of the movement, so that it should at least seem memorable – a small but determined force that stood as a radical alternative if the big parties were seen to fail.

This was true of both right- and left-wing radical movements.

The years 1925-29 were just such a period when there was no chance of any radical movement gaining power. After its shaky start, the Weimar Republic settled into a period of stability, reconstruction and reasonable prosperity. In this atmosphere even the Bavarian authorities had little time for trouble-makers, and following a single taste of inflammatory oratory on Hitler's part, he was banned from speaking for two years. Moreover, he obeyed the prohibition and in general behaved a good deal less provocatively than he had during the pre-putsch era. This line may have begun as a personal precaution against the possibility of being deported from Germany, of which he was not yet a citizen. But it soon developed into a consistent strategy of operating within the law and taking part in elections: while maintaining his brown-shirted private army, the SA, Hitler would use the despised parliamentary process to achieve power, with the unconcealed intention of *then* destroying the Republic and all its works.

With characteristically abrasive wording, Hitler told his followers that 'we must hold our noses' and take part in the democratic process.

Such a consummation seemed a distant prospect down to 1928, although the Nazis did at least establish a national (rather than exclusively Bavarian) organization. This was mainly the work of the brothers Gregor and Otto Strasser, whose strong revolutionary and anti-capitalist line led to conflicts with Hitler. It says a great deal for his personal magnetism and oratorical powers that, face to face with him when the party chiefs met at Bamberg in 1926, the Strassers succumbed and submitted – as, later on, most of his opponents within the party submitted.

In the general election of 1928 the Nazis polled a miserable 810,000 votes and sent only 12 representatives to the Reichstag. But they made a significant advance in the following year, when the Young Plan brought the issues of reparations and war-guilt back into the limelight. The Plan actually lowered the annual rate of reparations payments and entailed a French evacuation from the Rhineland; but it also opened old wounds, and the German Right mounted a concerted campaign against it. Alfred Hugenberg, leader of the main right-wing party, the Nationalists, was

Hitler the orator. The 'frenzied emotion' is deceptive: it was put on for the benefit of a photographer, who took the pictures so that Hitler could perfect his performances.

So much for the Nazi myth of a hideously powerful 'Jewish press'.

Plebiscite: national vote, taken to decide a single issue (i.e. not to decide which party should govern).

The Mark: the main unit of German currency.

Locarno and the Stresemann-Briand era: period of German-French reconciliation instituted by the Locarno treaties of 1925. Stresemann and Briand were the foreign ministers of Germany and France.

SS: black-uniformed Nazi elite guard which ultimately became a huge state security police.

'Marxist' parties: to Hitler and his followers both the Social Democrats (roughly equivalent to the British Labour Party) and the Communists were 'Marxists'. This was of course a smear tactic that was used before Hitler's day and has outlived him: it is still common to hear all left-of-centre parties labelled 'Red', just as all those on the right are sometimes denounced as 'fascists'.

sufficiently impressed by Hitler's gifts as a propagandist to join forces with him, financing the Nazis' share of the campaign and publicizing Hitler's activities in his far-flung press and film empire. After several months the campaign produced two important results: Hitler became a nationally known figure; and a plebiscite decisively supported Germany's acceptance of the Young Plan.

At the time, a shrewd observer might have predicted that the plebiscite was the result that mattered. The republican system was working, and people were not willing to risk its stability. Hitler's skill might bring the Nazis some future gains, but neither they nor any other radical force could hope to achieve power while the Weimar Republic provided its citizens with adequate workaday lives. Then the effects of the Great Depression began to be felt in Germany, and millions of lives ceased to be workaday, let alone adequate. In this situation, old resentments revived and many people began to look for a saviour with a radical solution. Thanks to the campaign against the Young Plan, Hitler was already present in the popular mind as a candidate-messiah, and profited accordingly. The Nazi vote in 1930-33 rose – and eventually fell – in tandem with the unemployment figures; and in fact

all through the fourteen years of struggling for power Hitler's ups and downs were in precisely inverse ratio to the prosperity of the country. His first bid for power in November 1923 happened on the very day on which inflation ($1 = 4.2 million million Marks) reached its absolute peak. A decline in the Party came at the time of Locarno and the Stresemann-Briand era envisaging 'prosperity round the corner'. With the economic crisis of the late 1920s the Party grew commensurate to ever more millions of unemployed, the 'peak' of the July elections coinciding with the peak of the dole statistics.

Roger Manvell and Heinrich Fraenkel, *The Hundred Days to Hitler*, Dent, 1974.

This highlights the extent to which the rise of Nazism was a social phenomenon rather than the result of political or propagandistic cleverness – although it can, of course, be argued that when matters came to a crisis these made the difference between success and failure. For, despite the Depression, Hitler's road to power was not a smooth one. The Nazis made their great breakthrough in the elections of September 1930, polling 6 million votes and increasing their Reichstag membership from 12 to 107. In July 1932 they reached their peak, with 13.74 million votes and 230 seats; over 37 per cent of Germans were now voting for Hitler.

These were years of frantic activity in which Hitler flew from city to city, making hundreds of speeches. As well as general elections there was a series of presidential, state and local contests that kept up the tension. Hitler was faced with many difficult decisions, of which the hardest followed the banning of the SA and the SS in April 1932. The SA now numbered hundreds of thousands of fighters who were thirsting for action and impatiently waiting for an end to Hitler's policy of legality – although, in the meantime, they waged war in the streets and broke up the meetings of the 'Marxist' parties. Yet Hitler's authority was such that he forced the SA to accept the ban, which was lifted only two months later. All the same, the longer the crisis lasted, the harder it was for Hitler to maintain the double image of National Socialism – as a right-wing movement that capitalists should fund as a bulwark against communism, and as a radical party which working people should support.

The most nerve-racking time of all began in the later months of 1932. For two years Germany had been ruled by presidential decrees issued by chancellors without a majority in the Reichstag. As the economic and

'Fighting the terror of the Left': the Nazi image of the storm trooper, whose street-fighting and breaking-up of other parties' meetings was passed off as 'self-defence'.

This too coincided with a change in the unemployment figures, this time for the better. (See the quotation on the opposite page.)

Gauleiter: Nazi official in charge of a Gau (district).

political crisis deepened, the conservative advisers around Hindenburg became anxious to bolster their position by bringing Hitler and his mass following into the government. But negotiations broke down several times because Hitler would accept nothing less than the chancellorship, whereas the conservatives wanted to harness Nazism, not submit to it. As time went on, Hitler's decision seemed increasingly dubious – especially after the elections of November 1932, when the Nazis experienced their first setback, losing some two million votes. The party's coffers were empty, and there were signs of mounting discontent. Unlike the conventional political parties, the NSDAP was always at full stretch, nerved for action – and therefore liable to disintegrate if it was kept waiting too long. As in 1923, there was a danger of mass desertions if Hitler failed to act. Should he attempt a putsch or make do with a share in power by accepting the vice-chancellorship for himself or a nominee? Gregor Strasser advocated power sharing, and in December 1932 the conservatives tried to split the Nazi movement by offering the vice-chancellorship to him. An enraged Hitler tackled Strasser head-on, and again Strasser made no attempt to resist or rally support against the Leader, although this time he resigned from the party and quit the political scene.

In self-justification Strasser argued that, if Hitler did not want to participate in government, he should lead a putsch: either option was better than inaction. Hitler expressed his own view at a meeting of Gauleiters, as one of those present recalled:

Whether or not he (Hitler) should accept the Vice-Chancellorship? Well obviously, within the first week there would have been insuperable differences with Chancellor Papen, who would have told him with a smile that if he did not like it he could go. What then could he report to their great Party and movement, which would break asunder giving the Communists their chance? He could not and would not enter the Government except as Chancellor; and that would happen soon enough. Everything else was as unrealistic as the 'illegal' measures envisaged by Strasser .... He quoted General Reichenau, who had complimented him on the Party's self-discipline and told him that if his storm-troops did 'march against law and order' the Army, albeit 'with a bleeding heart', would obey orders and shoot.
Gauleiter Lohse, quoted in Manvell and Fraenkel, *The Hundred Days to Hitler*.

Events soon justified Hitler's stand. The former chancellor, von Papen, had been ousted by General Schleicher; in January 1933 he obtained his revenge when Schleicher was forced out and Hitler and Hugenberg's Nationalists joined him in forming a new cabinet. But Hitler's price for the alliance had to be met, and on 30 January 1933 the National Socialist leader was formally appointed Chancellor of the Weimar Republic.

Since he succeeded, it is possible to say that Hitler had made the right decision – provided that we realize that bad or even stupid decisions can prove to be 'right' if an individual is lucky enough. A recent study argues that Hitler's obstinacy over the chancellorship was just such a decision – bad but lucky:

> . . . Hitler became German chancellor. Does this mean that Hitler's intransigent tactics had been right all along? Not necessarily. Hitler was rescued from the dead end of permanent opposition through a stroke of good fortune and despite his own obstinacy.
> Carr, *Hitler.*

The author goes on to argue that Hitler was saved because the leading German industrialists threw their weight behind him just in time, having concluded by late 1932 that Nazi economic policy offered the best prospects for surviving the Depression. If so, then it was Hitler's good luck that the industrialists did not take another few months to reach their decision – by which time the Nazi Party might have been in complete disarray.

Historians tend to prefer impersonal explanations – but is this anything more than a prejudice?

This makes Hitler's chancellorship the result of 'larger' forces rather than a series of squalid intrigues conducted around an almost senile President. But such an explanation implies that Hitler's confident anticipations had no rational basis. It can however be argued that the conservatives *had* to deal with Hitler, and that they could not afford to see the Nazi Party disintegrate. Only through the Nazis could the conservatives hope to rally mass support for nationalist values. Furthermore the NSDAP was not a traditional right-wing party, but included large numbers of embittered, radicalized individuals who, if disillusioned, would probably desert the Right and swing over to the other militant party – the Communists, who had also been steadily gaining in strength. This was a fearful prospect from a conservative point of view. Hitler may well have reasoned on this basis that he could afford to be obstinate, since they would be forced to come to terms 'soon enough'.

Moreover, the conservatives were running out of time, since their access to power depended on the survival of President Hindenburg, who was 85 years old.

But if Hitler's stance was rational, it was also surely inevitable. It is difficult to see how the supreme Leader, presented for years as a superman, could become the junior partner in a reactionary government. Or how this could be done after Hitler had so often boasted that his purpose was not to play Ins and Outs with ministries, like ordinary politicians, but to create a revolutionary new National Socialist order. And what would he have done to placate the SA, already straining at the leash and loot-hungry? Even if we discount Hitler's own personality, with its penchant for absolute decisions, this seems to be an instance in which his tactics were not only 'right' but were determined by the very nature of the movement he led.

The Dictator

Remodelling the Reich

Franz von Papen (1879-1969), ex-chancellor whose intrigues were mainly responsible for bringing Hitler to power (see above).

'We've tamed him!' Or so von Papen, Hitler's vice-chancellor, is supposed to have remarked after the formation of the new German cabinet. As a result of the negotiations the Nazis had to be content with only three cabinet seats out of eleven, so the conservatives appeared to be justified in believing that they could control Hitler and employ his unruly followers as guardians of the traditional aristocratic-military order. They failed to appreciate the use that could be made of key positions such as Hitler's chancellorship and Göring's control of the police as Prussian prime minister; and they had no real conception of the ruthlessness and momentum of Nazism, a movement whose true values were quite alien to those of officers and gentlemen.

Events moved with extraordinary rapidity. On 27 February the Reichstag was gutted by fire. To this day it is not clear whether the culprit, an unhinged young Dutchman named van der Lubbe, acted alone or was manipulated by the Nazis: what is certain is that the fire was used as an excuse to persecute the Communists, panic the electorate, and give Hitler's government sweeping emergency powers. In the election campaign that followed, state control over the police and the media was invariably used to favour Hitler and his allies. On 5 March, at the end of a singularly violent campaign, the Nazis had polled 43.9 per cent of the votes – a big advance, but less than might have been expected in such favourable circumstances. Any generalization about 'the Germans' must take into account the fact that a majority of them never voted for Hitler while they were offered a choice.

But, as Hitler had already promised, this was to be 'the last election'. With the help of their allies and a little double-dealing, the Nazis commanded the two-thirds majority in the Reichstag which they needed to pass the notorious Enabling Act. This gave Hitler dictatorial powers – including the power to change the constitution – for a period of four years. Paradoxically, a tyranny was set up with due respect for legal and constitutional forms. It was even perpetuated legally by renewals of the Enabling Act every four years – so that, in a sense, Hitler's policy of legality was followed right through to the end of the Third Reich.

Within four months all political parties except the NSDAP had been banned or (like Hugenberg's Nationalists) had accepted the inevitable and dissolved themselves. Mass arrests were made, and concentration camps were set up to hold Communists and other undesirables. Bavaria and other states effectively surrendered their independence, so that the federal Weimar Republic was replaced by the highly centralized Third Reich. The trade unions were taken over, and the press, book publishing and other media brought under strict control. Soon education was Nazified, and huge public bonfires of books prevented German minds from being corrupted by Jewish, liberal, left-wing, sexually unconventional, pacifist, feminist and other 'unhealthy' works. In characteristic totalitarian fashion, even science and art were subject to ideological control: 'Jewish science', personified by Einstein, was cast out, and modernism in painting and sculpture was condemned as 'degenerate art'.

Hitler himself was surprised by the speed with which the political parties gave up the ghost. Indeed, the lack of resistance to *Gleichschaltung* – the policy of 'co-ordinating' or 'bringing into line' all the institutions of the former republic – suggests that people had finally become numbed by the tensions of the previous few years, and perhaps even felt a sense of relief that Germany's fate had been decided.

Nor was this just Hitler's doing. He needed able assistants at all times, but never more so than when taking over the state machinery. Historians agree that

In the critical period of 1933-4, no man after Hitler played so important a role in

Prussia was easily the largest German state, the key to controlling the entire Reich.

The instructions issued by Göring (page 36) indicate the licence allowed to the police and the SA.

Albert Einstein (1879-1955) whose theory of relativity revolutionized physics.

Herman Göring, until the early 1940s Hitler's principal lieutenant. Often seen as a figure of fun (he grew enormously fat), he was in reality able and utterly lacking in scruples.

the Nazi revolution as Göring. His energy and ruthlessness, together with his control of Prussia, were indispensable to Hitler's success.
Bullock, *Hitler*.

Even before the election Göring dismissed thousands of politically suspect police and civil servants, brought in 50,000 SA men as auxiliary police and set up the Gestapo. On 17 February he issued a notorious order making it clear that the police must 'thoroughly support' the 'national' forces during the campaign, whereas

Gestapo: secret state police, not to be confused with the uniformed SS.

the activities of organizations hostile to the State are to be checked by the strongest methods. With Communist terrorism and raids there must be no trifling, and, when necessary, revolvers must be used without regard to consequences. Police officers who fire their revolvers in the execution of their duties will be protected by me without regard to the consequences of using their weapons. But officials who fail, out of mistaken regard for consequences, must expect disciplinary action to be taken against them.
Quoted in Manvell and Fraenkel, *The Hundred Days to Hitler*.

This is typical of Göring in its relish for proclaiming a complete lack of scruple. Although the subject of this book is Hitler, such a passage is a useful reminder that he was surrounded by men who were not mere tools but willing collaborators. Hitler was the Nazis' master, but Nazism was nevertheless a social phenomenon that cannot be summed up in the history of one man.

To say that Nazism was a social phenomenon does not necessarily mean that Hitler's specific personality made no difference to its history. See page 61.

What kind of dictator?

Nor was Hitler the kind of dictator who tries to know everything and do everything. Where his main interests – diplomacy and war – were concerned, he could work incessantly; but he had little interest in administrative problems, and was content to delegate a great deal of authority to his subordinates. In fact it is surprising how successfully Hitler managed to maintain his old bohemian life-style during the pre-war years,

Dr Joseph Goebbels, second only to his Führer as a propagandist; master of 'the Big Lie'.

The quality of Hitler's decision-making is another matter over which historians disagree. His subordinates were often agitated by his apparent inability to decide, or by orders given and then countermanded; and some historians have bluntly described this as dithering. Hitler, of course, claimed that he knew how to wait until the right moment, when the proper course of action became clear. Probably the only way to resolve the issue is by evaluating the decisions themselves.

Also known as 'the Blood Purge'. Such high-flown, 'heroic' language was part of the texture of Nazism.

rising at midday and talking late into the night with his cronies, fleeing from Berlin (which he disliked) for long weekends at his Bavarian mountain retreat at Berchtesgaden, and alternating between dreaming over grandiose schemes (whether architectural or 'world historical') and bouts of intense activity.

However, this was not necessarily a weakness. The ability to delegate authority is generally recognized as a positive quality in a leader, allowing him or her the time needed for large-scale planning and major decisions. What matters is that the subordinates should be men of ability, and that any intervention by the leader should carry the stamp of authority. As far as ability is concerned it would be difficult to prove conclusively that Hitler's henchmen were less efficient in their own way than the members of a British cabinet; and no one doubts that Hitler's interventions were decisive in political matters.

In fact Hitler allowed and even encouraged the development of rival 'empires' inside the Third Reich, giving his principal lieutenants wide but usually overlapping responsibilities. As a result, men such as Göring and Himmler, Goebbels and Rosenberg, intrigued against one another and were constantly complaining and appealing to Hitler – a situation calculated to emphasize his supremacy. Historians have commented severely on the structural incoherence of the Reich, and the jobbery and corruption to which it gave rise, although it is not so easy to demonstrate their adverse effects, at least in peacetime. As we shall see, pre-war Nazi Germany seemed an admirably run state to many observers. But it is now clear that the popular image of the Nazi state – as a streamlined machine driven by a single fanatical will – is quite wide of the mark.

Rivalries between leading Nazis played a part in the sensational 'Night of the Long Knives' of 30 June 1934. There had always been antagonism between the political and paramilitary branches of the NSDAP, and Göring and Goebbels certainly did their best to persuade Hitler that the SA were planning a putsch. Although this was a fabrication, the SA did represent an unsatisfied element in the Nazi ranks. Since 1931 it had been commanded by Hitler's old associate, Ernst Röhm, who wanted to take the Nazi revolution a stage further by merging the SA – now over three million strong – with the army. This possibility outraged the conservatives, whom Hitler was trying to conciliate, and raised the spectre of conflict between the army and the Nazis. True to his strategy of winning over the authorities,

Hitler chose the army: on the night of 30 June Röhm and other SA leaders were arrested and shot, along with a number of other people (Gregor Strasser, General Schleicher, Bavarian State Commissioner von Kahr) who had crossed swords with the Führer in the past.

Hitler seems to have been genuinely distressed by the need to eliminate his old companion-in-arms Röhm – indeed, military-style comradeship was arguably the form of personal relationship that meant most to him. But characteristically he extracted the maximum political benefit from the crisis. Germany's most prestigious institution, the army, adopted the swastika banner and effectively endorsed the National Socialist state; it retained much of its independence for some years, but the process of infiltrating and subduing it had begun. And Hitler did not hesitate to claim that, faced with an emergency, he had acted outside the law, as Germany's supreme judge. This assertion, approved by his conservative colleagues, foreshadowed the Nazification of the legal system and raised the Führer himself to still more godlike heights. When President Hindenburg died in December 1934, the offices of president and chancellor were combined in the single person of Adolf Hitler.

Nevertheless, over the next few years Hitler proceeded with caution. The Night of the Long Knives had harmed Nazi Germany's international image and disturbed many Germans, but between 1934 and 1938 the damage was made good. Germany gave an impression of being prosperous and orderly, and those who wished to could believe that Hitler was becoming respectable. One example of his political shrewdness is seen in his dealings with the Christian churches. Although heroic individuals – pastors and priests as well as laymen – opposed Nazism, the churches as such remained quiescent. But when enthusiastic Nazis who called themselves 'German-Christians' tried to take over and 'Aryanize' the Protestant church, there was a vigorous reaction – and Hitler hastily reined in his supporters. Later, especially during the Second World War, many pastors who had opposed him would end their lives in concentration camps or on the gallows; and no doubt a day of reckoning with the churches would have arrived if the war had not been lost. In the meantime Hitler preferred not to jeopardize his popularity at home or his status abroad by direct attacks on the churches.

What, then, of his treatment of the Jews? Immediate steps were taken to reduce their numbers in the civil service and education; the 1935 Nuremberg Racial Laws excluded Jews from German citizenship; and the notorious 1938 Crystal Night outraged world opinion. Many writers have

Reliable information about Hitler's personal life is meagre indeed. He appears to have been devastated by the suicide of his adored neice, Geli Raubal, in 1931. But it is not even clear whether she killed herself because of Hitler's attentions or because he had taken Eva Braun as his mistress. Neither woman is known to have influenced him politically.

There are various controversies concerning the role of the churches, notably the failure of Popes Pius XI and Pius XII (ardent opponents of communism) to denounce Nazism and the persecution of the Jews. Such issues are outside the scope of this book, which aims to investigate Hitler's actions and reactions.

Crystal Night: the 'Night of Breaking Glass', government-stimulated anti-semitic rioting and shop-smashing, accompanied by many murders.

A new image: Hitler the respectable statesman. His appearances on public occasions with war hero President Hindenburg (centre) were taken to mean that the old Imperial Germany gave its blessing to the new National Socialist Third Reich.

Triumphant propaganda celebrates the Nazis' victory and derides their victims. (Left) Germany does her spring cleaning and sweeps away the Communists; (Right) 'yes' to Nazism alarms the Jews.

pointed out that, merely in terms of political advantage, anti-semitism was a dubious policy, since it gave the regime a bad name abroad and drove out some 300,000 industrious members of the community (including scientists whose work might later have made all the difference to the war effort). One modern writer (Ronald Lewin) has suggested that after the Night of the Long Knives Hitler could have blamed the SA for earlier violence against the Jews and pursued a more moderate policy, merely restricting Jewish civil rights. Well, why not? After all,

> As he [Hitler] was utterly without principles, the alteration or abandonment of apparently fixed and sacred policies caused him no qualms.
> Ronald Lewin, *Hitler's Mistakes*, Cooper, 1984.

Among these 'fixed and sacred policies', Lewin points out, was anti-Bolshevism – which did not prevent Hitler from making a non-aggression pact with the USSR in 1939. However, this argument is not altogether convincing, since the Nazi-Soviet Pact was simply a short-term tactic on Hitler's part: less than two years later he launched a massive, unprovoked and ultimately fatal attack on the USSR.

Evidently his 'principles' were of some consequence after all. And of these anti-semitism was probably the strongest. For, as pointed out earlier, the hatred of the Jews expressed in *Mein Kampf* has an eerily personal, pathological quality that would have cost Hitler more effort to overcome than a political principle. (It could even be argued that his pre-war treatment of the Jews *was* restrained and discreet – by his standards.)

The issue raised here is a fundamental one. Was Hitler 'utterly without principles' in pursuit of power, or did he follow 'fixed and sacred policies' despite apparent contradictions and detours for tactical purposes? The

See page 28.

If your impulse is to annihilate, it shows a certain restraint if you only persecute.

Projecting a benevolent image: young worshippers seek the Führer's autograph and are not disappointed.

Most contemporary observers thought so. But of course opposition tends to be invisible in a police state.

reader's conclusion on this point is bound to affect the way in which all Hitler's policies are interpreted.

Germany remade?

Once in power, the Nazis seem to have been extremely successful in convincing Germans that Hitler was introducing a great new era of national reconciliation. Just as the political parties surrendered in 1933 as though morally vanquished, all sorts of groups – including academics and intellectuals – hurried to pledge their allegiance long before it was required of them. Despite bad moments such as the Röhm Purge, in the early years of power Hitler was borne along by a surge of national confidence and enthusiasm.

Two important factors were a sense of relief that things were settled at last, and optimism generated by signs of economic recovery, which had begun to appear at the end of 1932. In this favourable atmosphere Nazi propaganda was brilliantly effective in making people believe that Germany was again 'on the move', with a splendid future in front of her.

More image-making. Hitler was often photographed with children and dogs to emphasize his 'human' side.

Propaganda was one of the Nazis' most potent weapons, and in this sphere Hitler was supreme. He was ably assisted by men such as Dr Joseph Goebbels, his Minister of National Enlightenment and Propaganda; but, whether designing the swastika flag or making speeches, Hitler was the master.

Hitler also supplied all the party's basic ideas about propaganda in *Mein Kampf*; on this subject, at least his writing is incisive and still intensely interesting. The masses have short memories and do not understand argument, Hitler asserts: give them one or two simple slogans, repeated again and again and again until they sink in and are believed. Nor are the masses concerned with ideas and principles: they are attracted to strength, and will gravitate towards a movement that seems charged with such brute force that nothing can stop it. Hence the slogans, the uniforms, banners, torchlight processions, and so on of the Nazi Party before Hitler took power; and the even more spectacular stage effects afterwards, especially on occasions such as the Nuremberg Rallies. Even the street-fighting of the storm-troopers before 1933 was intended as a demonstration of Nazi strength and will, though it is arguable that it always offended the respectable and would certainly have been counter-productive in more settled times. But once sanctioned by the state, the power and will exhibited through Nazi propaganda made a deep appeal – and not only to Germany in the 1930s, for books and films about the Nazis continue to entice European and American audiences. In part, at least, this is probably because

> the regime satisfied to a high degree the craving for adventure, heroic dedication, and that gambler's passion in which Hitler shared and for which modern social-welfare states leave so little room.
> Fest, *Hitler*.

Nazi propaganda also influenced foreigners – those, for example, who saw the classic documentary film *Triumph of the Will*, recording the impressively

Can you suggest why readers of Mein Kampf were not offended by his contempt for the masses?

It could be argued that Fest does not go far enough – that commitment to Nazism 'cured' such recognized ills of modern life as isolation, alienation and a sense of impotence.

Not for publication: Hitler with his long-time companion Eva Braun, who stayed very much in the background. Neither she nor any other women in Hitler's private life seem to have influenced his political actions.

Many distinguished foreigners sympathized with the new Germany. (Can you name any British or American examples?) They were often influenced by anti-communism and a belief that Germany had been unfairly treated at Versailles. But even people like Winston Churchill admired the way in which Hitler had 'restored Germany's self-respect' – an understandable reaction in a world whose highest political value was 'national greatness'.

Autobahn: motorway. Such motorways would not be seen in Britain for another twenty-odd years.

Autarchy: self-sufficiency, achieved, e.g., by diversifying production and developing synthetic substitutes for materials not produced at home.

orchestrated 1934 Nuremberg Rally, or visited Germany for such prestige events as the 1936 Olympic Games in Berlin. And although the Nazis were skilful at window-dressing for the benefit of the outside world, the regime did have some important achievements to its credit. Above all, mass unemployment was ended; and although various objections and qualifications have been put forward by economists and others, the fact remains that Hitler quickly solved a problem which had baffled – and continued to baffle – the leaders of other industrialized nations. The most important measure was to set people to work on public projects and pay them. This meant that they could start spending; which in turn meant that shops and factories took on workers and started producing more goods and services to meet the renewed demand; as a result conditions began to return to normal. By 'printing money' and distributing it, the government got the economic machinery working again: the process is comparable to pushing a car along to get its engine turning over.

In Germany the public works included useful projects (notably the Autobahns), but increasingly the expenditure was on rearmament, which was of course intended to further Hitler's foreign policy aims. The 'economic miracle' on the home front interlocked neatly with the concerns described in *Mein Kampf*.

As early as 1936 the interlocking was less neat, and the pace of rearmament began to put a severe strain on the German economy. Hitler was faced with crucial alternatives, and his choice is prime evidence that he meant what he had written in *Mein Kampf*. Rearmament would go on. A policy of autarchy would economize on spending abroad, enabling surplus foreign exchange to be spent on vital food and materials. Hitler's own memorandum on the subject proposes 'an extension of our living-space' as the eventual solution, bringing Germany the foodstuffs and raw materials that she needed. The memorandum concludes:

I thus set the following tasks: I. The German armed forces must be operational within four years. II. The German economy must be fit for war within four years.
Quoted in most biographies of Hitler.

Spectacular displays of German might were a Nazi speciality. At this Nuremburg Rally of 1936 the flood-lighting overawed observers, who were not to know that every last anti-aircraft searchlight in the Reich had been brought to the city in order to create an impression of vast resources.

1938: German troops enter Austria, greeted by crowds waving Nazi flags.

Whether this economic policy ever became totally irreversible is not so clear. To what extent has excessive spending on armaments driven the present-day superpowers to war-like courses?

'Rump' Czechoslovakia: the part of Czechoslovakia left after her cessions of territory to Germany, Hungary and Poland after the Munich agreement (page 47).

In other words, Germany's economic problems were not to be solved by economic adjustments, but by diplomatic-military action. As a result of this decision the economy would become increasingly lopsided, making it more difficult every year to pull back from an expansionist policy, even if Hitler had wished to do so. His foreign policy during the 1930s could therefore be said to represent a choice which turned into something approaching a necessity.

Master diplomatist?

All of this fits in with the traditional picture of Hitler as committed to an eastern expansionist policy which would risk a conflict with Britain and France, and would certainly culminate in war with the USSR. In the 1940s many people even believed that Hitler had followed a blueprint or timetable for expansion, especially from 1938, when his coups occurred with what seemed a planned regularity in spring and autumn (annexation of Austria; dismemberment of Czechoslovakia; destruction of 'rump' Czechoslovakia; invasion of Poland). After the Second World War, when Hitler's surviving henchmen were put on trial at Nuremberg, one of the most serious charges brought against them was that of 'planning aggressive war'.

This view was persuasively challenged by the English historian A.J.P. Taylor in his *Origins of the Second World War* (1961). Taylor's book has already become a classic: that is, a work of such force and skill that it can delight a reader who totally disagrees with it. Though dated in some respects, it remains an influential and provocative alternative to the received view of Hitler.

Taylor believes that statesmen's books, articles and other off-duty statements should be taken with a very large pinch of salt: they are 'daydreams', doubtless sincere but hardly relevant to action in the real world:

> In my opinion, statesmen are too absorbed by events to follow a preconceived plan. They take one step, and the next follows from it. The systems are created by historians, as happened with Napoleon; and the systems attributed to Hitler are really those of Hugh Trevor-Roper, Elizabeth Wiskemann, and Alan Bullock.
> Taylor, *Origins of the Second World War.*

On this view, Hitler was essentially a political opportunist, taking his advantages where he could find them. There was no blueprint or timetable, and many of his master-strokes were in fact hastily improvised. For example, Austria was annexed because her chancellor, Schuschnigg, tried to go back on his agreement with Hitler by holding a plebiscite that the Nazis were bound to lose; so Hitler, at bay, was virtually compelled to retaliate with the threats and telephone diplomacy that broke Schuschnigg's resistance.

Moreover in rearming Germany – never as rapidly as contemporaries believed – Hitler was just doing what the statesmen of other powers do: arming in order to put 'muscle' behind his diplomacy, and preparing for the possibility of a war without necessarily intending to fight one. Even the existence of war plans and directives prove nothing, since all nations play war games and make contingency plans.

Taylor's other main argument is that, as a diplomatist, Hitler was not much different from any other German statesman. There was nothing specific to Hitler in a wish to destroy the Versailles settlement and bring all Germans into the Reich. And if that happened Germany would inevitably become the dominant European power – a possibility that constituted the basic 'German problem', whether or not Adolf Hitler was at the helm of the state. Yes, Taylor writes, Hitler was responsible for acts of immeasurable evil; but that is not relevant here, since

> His foreign policy was a different matter. He aimed to make Germany the dominant Power in Europe and maybe, more remotely, in the world. Other Powers have pursued similar aims, and still do. Other Powers treat smaller countries as their satellites. Other Powers seek to defend their vital interests by force of arms. In international affairs there was nothing wrong with Hitler except that he was a German.
> Taylor, 'Second Thoughts', Foreword to *Origins*, 2nd edition, 1963.

Taylor raises many points that are worth bearing in mind when studying history, whether or not you agree with the way he applies them to Hitler's policies during the 1930s. The subject is a wide and intricate one, and here we can only touch on a few considerations brought into focus by Taylor's book.

There are many objections to the notion that, in foreign affairs, Hitler was not much different from earlier German leaders. To begin with, his policies were 'continental', not concerned with colonies, as pre-war governments had been. Furthermore, conquests to provide living-space in

But when a man says he will achieve certain ends and then achieves them ... it is surely possible that this was not a coincidence!

Three well-known historians of the Hitler period.

But obviously statesmen can have *goals* without laying down a timetable for their achievement.

In Taylor's view, historians merely voice their prejudices when they attempt to distinguish between 'aggressive' German and 'defensive' British planning.

Was Hitler a run-of-the-mill German (or European) diplomatist in his conception of 'vital interests'?

the east had never been a German aim, although the First World War victories over Russia at one time held out the prospect of huge annexations; but even then, enslavement of the natives and settlement by German 'masters' was never on the agenda. Attempting to strengthen his case, Taylor in fact gives it away when he contends that Hitler simply acted out the loosely held, only half-serious ideas held by his fellow-countrymen because he was 'terrifyingly literal-minded' in pursuing his hatred of Jews, contempt for Slavs etc. For this is only another way of saying that he *was* different from other German leaders, who did not believe in such ideas strongly enough to act on them, if indeed they believed them at all.

Only in the more limited, strictly post-war aims of 'rescuing' the Germans of Czechoslovakia and Poland, and bringing about a union with Austria, is there an element of continuity between the Weimar and Nazi outlooks. Even German statesmen such as Gustav Stresemann, the apostle of international reconciliation, privately hoped to achieve these goals in time, though by traditional methods of diplomacy. But since methods also count for something when we discuss continuities, it should be said that Hitler's high-risk, breakneck-speed foreign policy represented a complete breech with previous German – or even European – diplomacy. Whether its gains could have been made in any way but Hitler's – by bluffing, gambling and threats – is another matter.

During the first year or two of the Nazi regime, when Germany was visibly weak, Hitler's foreign policy was cautious. It began resoundingly with Germany's withdrawal from the League of Nations and from a disarmament conference which rejected her claims to parity. Then, despite the potentially explosive issues of Danzig and the German minority in Poland, Hitler concluded a non-aggression pact with Poland that secured Germany from danger on one front and began the erosion of French influence in Eastern Europe. But in July 1934, when Austrian Nazis attempted to stage a coup in Vienna, the stationing of Italian forces on the Brenner Pass was sufficient to persuade Hitler that the time was not ripe for intervention.

In March 1935 Hitler denounced the clauses of the Versailles settlement limiting the size of Germany's armed forces; conscription was introduced and plans for an army of 36 divisions set on foot. The other great powers protested but took no effective action. They knew that the Germans had been evading the Versailles requirements for years, even under the Weimar Republic, and they were inclined to believe that Hitler was simply announcing the formidable strength that he already possessed:

> It was not until 1935 that the full terror of this revelation broke upon the careless and imprudent world, and Hitler, casting aside concealment, sprang forward armed to the teeth, with his munitions factories roaring night and day, his aeroplane squadrons forming in ceaseless succession, his submarine crews exercising in the Baltic, and his armed hosts tramping the barrack squares from one end of the broad Reich to the other.
> Winston S. Churchill, 'Hitler and his Choice, 1935'; in *Great Contemporaries*, Macmillan, 1937.

Modern research has shown that this was a delusion. German rearmament was a reality but not an overnight process, and in 1935-6 Germany would still have been no match for France. Hitler's generals told him so in March 1936, when he contemplated a march into the demilitarized Rhineland. It went ahead because Hitler was confident that the French would not fight, whether through 'decadence' or a will-sapping conviction that Germany was only recovering territory that was legitimately hers.

But by Taylor's own criteria, Stresemann's private hopes are irrelevant: in practice his foreign policy was utterly different from Hitler's.

Since Churchill became the principal British opponent of Chamberlain's appeasement policy (page 14), it is interesting to note that his view of the Nazi menace was partly based on a misconception of German strength. Yet few people would now deny that Churchill *had* intuitively grasped Hitler's outlook and intentions.

Luftwaffe: German air force.

The treaty cost Hitler nothing, since he had no ambitions beyond Europe at the time.

No doubt the impression of German strength and resolution played its part. Unlike most statesmen, Hitler exaggerated rather than minimized the force at his command: Nazi propaganda created the impression that the German people had become an ant-like army, obedient to a single will, and specific, quite false claims – for example, that the Luftwaffe had achieved parity with the RAF – were shamelessly advanced and naively accepted by foreign governments and their advisers. Hitler was therefore able to negotiate from the appearance of strength even before the strength had been created.

It was also characteristic that he should follow up a belligerent action with a conciliatory gesture. Three months after the march into the Rhineland, the Anglo-German naval agreement committed Germany not to exceed 35 per cent of Britain's naval forces. Britain was reassured on the point that mattered most to her – her naval supremacy – at some cost to her relations with France, although the German-British-Italian alliance that Hitler hoped for was never to materialize. Making a bold forward move and then talking of peace and announcing peace proposals became a favourite tactic of Hitler's. The effect was to throw any but the most resolute antagonist off balance, tempting him to accept a *fait accompli* and look for security in the new state of affairs. Hitler employed comparable tactics when negotiating, throwing one of his famous rages (which he seems to have turned on and off at will) when expected to get down to facts, then becoming 'reasonable' and charming just when everyone else was keyed up for conflict. With statesmen and diplomatists of the old school these psychological tactics were, at least in the short term, remarkably effective.

Although Britain's partnership with France was never seriously breached, Italy did become more and more firmly aligned with Nazi Germany, despite Mussolini's initial suspicions of Hitler. By contrast, Hitler had always admired the Italian dictator and had to some extent taken him as a model. But what bound them together was not ideology or friendship, but the fact that both Italy and Germany were expansionist or 'have-not' powers: both would engage in adventures that alienated the

The other Austrians, for whom union with Germany was not such good news: elderly Jews being forced to scrub a pavement while gleeful Nazis look on.

'haves' (Britain and France), and it was therefore natural for them to form a common front. The German-Italian 'Axis' was in existence by 1936, and became a formal alliance, the Pact of Steel, in May 1939.

By the spring of 1938 it had become clear that Italy, the only great power in a position to protect Austria, would no longer do so. Intense German pressure was brought to bear on Austria, and her chancellor, Schuschnigg, agreed to make Austria a German dependant with an ominously large share in the government given to Austrian Nazis. As we have seen, Schuschnigg attempted to wriggle out of the agreement by holding a snap plebiscite, and it was this that brought on a decisive intervention that incorporated Austria in the Third Reich. In a sense, therefore, the Anschluss was not planned but, as A.J.P. Taylor argues, improvised. On the other hand, the improvisation took place in the context of a campaign whose ultimate purpose was quite clear. So most historians would argue that Hitler's ability to improvise was not at all incompatible with his determination to achieve certain long-term fixed aims.

See page 44.

Moreover the relentless tempo of Hitler's foreign policy indicates that, even if he had no 'timetable', he certainly intended to achieve his aims in the very near future. Two weeks after the Anschluss, he was instructing the Sudeten German leader, Konrad Henlein, to intensify his agitation against Czech rule. Both men were quite clear that the objective was not merely to secure justice for Germans in Czechoslovakia. On the contrary: 'We should always demand so much that we can never be satisfied' was their agreed course of action. From the beginning Hitler hoped to undermine the Czech state, capitalizing on the grievances of the Sudetens through intensive propaganda and deliberate subversion, while preparing a lightning attack on Czechoslovakia.

However, in two dramatic flights to meet Hitler, the British prime minister, Neville Chamberlain, tried to head off a war. He made it clear that Britain and France were willing to see the Sudetenland become part of the Reich, and had compelled the Czechs to consent to the transfer. Yet when Chamberlain announced this on his second visit, Hitler abruptly increased his demands. The British and French stood firm, and for a few days war seemed imminent. Then Hitler was persuaded to take part in a four power conference at Munich on 29-30 September 1938, which gave him the Sudetenland.

France, not Britain, was bound by treaty to aid the Czechs if they were attacked, and this may be why the French allowed Chamberlain to take the principal role in negotiating with Hitler; they could then claim that British policy left them no alternative but the abandonment of Czechoslovakia.

Why did Hitler risk a European war when he could gain so much in complete safety? Most historians think he wanted to fight and destroy Czechoslovakia; and it is certainly true that both before and after the

Hitler, British prime minister Neville Chamberlain and Nazi foreign minister Ribbentrop inspect a guard of honour at Munich airport. Having agreed that Germany should annexe Czechoslovakia's Sudetenland area, Chamberlain returned to Britain believing that he had arranged 'peace in our time'.

Munich agreement he claimed to feel cheated of his prey. If this view is correct, he may have been persuaded to settle by the notable lack of enthusiasm for war among the German population, and by the German generals' misgivings about breaking through Czechoslovakia's powerful border fortifications. Other historians (principally A.J.P. Taylor) have argued that, by pressing Polish and Hungarian claims on Czech territory, Hitler hoped to precipitate the disintegration of the state. On this view, Hitler behaved perfectly rationally, gaining a little extra time in which events might bring him further gains while remaining ready to settle if this failed to happen. Both interpretations imply a powerful urge to destroy the Czech state, and tend to discredit the idea that Hitler was a diplomatist in the ordinary mould.

The destruction was postponed, not averted. After Munich, Czechoslovakia was subjected to one German demand after another, and a separatist movement among the Slovaks was given every German encouragement. The writing was clearly on the wall for the Czechs, and the situation soon offered Hitler the opportunity he was looking for. When the Czech government acted to put down Slovak unrest, the Slovak leader, Tiso, was summoned to Berlin and presented with a Slovak declaration of independence that he was expected to endorse and put out as his own! Since the Slovaks dared not risk the loss of German patronage, they duly acted as Hitler wished. Now, having promoted the disintegration of Czechoslovakia, Hitler could use it as an excuse to send in troops to 'restore order'. Just before they marched, Hacha, the president of Czechoslovakia, asked for an interview with Hitler. His visit proved to be a bonus, since he eventually signed a statement in which he 'confidently placed the fate of the Czech people in the hands of the Führer'; no mention was made of the German forces already on the move. Since Czechoslovakia was doomed anyway, Hacha's action saved Czech lives; but it also enabled Hitler to act with perfect legality in turning Czechoslovakia into German 'protectorates'.

It seems worth pointing out here that the Nazis (not necessarily Hitler himself) developed most of the devious tactics characteristic of modern international politics – internal subversion by subsidized minorities, faked appeals for German intervention, false reports of enemy atrocities and fabricated 'incidents'. Indispensable modern instruments of Hitlerian diplomacy were the telephone and the aeroplane, without which the fast tempo of 1938–9 would have been impossible. Neville Chamberlain can be credited with the invention of a more well-intentioned modern phenomenon, shuttle diplomacy.

As a result of the Munich agreement, these fortifications were handed over to Germany without a fight.

Another state friendly to Hitler – Hungary – had its eyes on Slovak territory.

Hacha was subjected to intense psychological pressure and actually had a (non-fatal) heart attack during the proceedings.

These tactics have made it difficult to be sure whether an act of aggression has taken place – and, if it has, whether or not the aggression was unprovoked.

What Munich meant to the Sudetenland: a shop front daubed with swastikas, and Czech words on the shop sign crudely obliterated.

National Socialist caring: Hitler, Goebbels and Göring considering plans for the Winter Relief appeal. The group is glamorized in the style of contemporary Hollywood studio photography.

Despite its German majority, Memel had been awarded to Lithuania after the First World War – in German eyes, another of the injustices perpetrated at Versailles.

Poland's government too was authoritarian, anti-Soviet and anti-semitic.

Officially the League of Nations was responsible for Danzig (hence the inhabitants were able to elect a Nazi administration). But by 1939 the League was impotent and only the Poles stood in the way of the city's return to the Reich.

Having guaranteed Poland, Britain and France had no means of putting pressure on her to compromise. Unlike the Czechs, the Poles knew – or thought they knew – that they would not have to fight alone.

Immediately after the destruction of Czechoslovakia, Lithuania was forced to cede Memel to Germany. There was no doubt that its inhabitants wanted this; but the way in which Hitler conducted the negotiations, browbeating the Lithuanians with the now familiar take-it-or-else instant deadline, strengthened the impression that German grievances merely provided an excuse for the Führer to go on the rampage – especially since he was already beginning a new agitation against Poland.

Britain and France had begun to draw this conclusion even before the German occupation of Bohemia and Moravia. They speeded up their rearmament programmes and issued guarantees to Poland and other East European states that the western democracies would intervene if the independence of these states was threatened. The British and French were far from despairing of peace, and were not even opposed to the Poles making concessions, but they were now beginning to feel that Hitler could not be allowed to keep on annexing entire states.

At first Hitler's intentions towards the Poles may have been relatively friendly. Throughout the 1930s, good relations between Nazi Germany and Poland had been maintained, and the Poles had actually taken part in the dismemberment of Czechoslovakia. By Hitler's standards, his demands on them were modest: the Free City of Danzig, which already had an elected Nazi administration, must return to the Reich, and Germany must be allowed to build road and rail links across the Polish Corridor to isolated East Prussia. Then perhaps Poland would march with Germany against the common enemy – Soviet Russia.

If this was Hitler's original plan, it broke down in the face of Poland's resolve to yield nothing and to remain independent of both her powerful neighbours. Subsequently, aggressive Nazi propaganda, including charges of 'atrocities' committed against the German minority in Poland, made absolutely no difference. Having seen the results of appeasement in Czechoslovakia's fate – and perhaps overrating their own strength – the Poles refused to contemplate concessions.

Most historians agree that this made a European war almost inevitable. Britain and France were committed to support Poland; and if the Poles refused to negotiate with Hitler, he must either give up all his demands or risk a general war. There was never any serious doubt about his decision. Hitler's need to maintain his prestige, his expansionist ideology, his own

2. THE STORY OF CRUEL ADOLF

Here is cruel Adolf, see!
A horrid wicked boy was he;
He made a purge to serve his end,
And shot up all his oldest friends.
He killed the little neutral birds
And always broke his plighted words.
He crushed poor Pussy, tore each pact
And screamed until his voice was cracked,
And urged with blows poor Madame France
To help him on her neighbour dance.

Even during the war, hostile commentators in the democracies emphasized the ridiculous side of Hitler – possibly an error, even from a propaganda point of view. Here he is 'cruel Adolf' in a reworked version of a well-known German children's story.

But A.J.P. Taylor believes that Hitler was simply a day out in his timing, and that there would otherwise have been a settlement.

A non-aggression pact commits the parties not to attack each other. It is not an alliance, since neither power is obliged to assist the other if it should go to war with a third party.

temperament and the momentum of success all combined to drive him forward. As early as May 1939 he told his service chiefs that Danzig was not the objective, and that he intended to attack Poland at the first favourable opportunity. Whether or not he would have been contented with a new Munich-style settlement will never be known. He certainly hoped to the last that the British and French would let the Poles down, or would make peace after Poland had been smashed and honour had been satisfied by a bloodless 'phoney war' in the west.

Hitler's final pre-war coup sheds a good deal of light on his intentions. Despite her ferociously anti-Soviet outlook, Nazi Germany abruptly concluded a non-aggression pact with the USSR on 23 August 1939. Once decided upon, the negotiations had been rushed through, and at one point Hitler himself had urgently telegraphed the Soviet leader, Stalin, in order to clear away the remaining obstacles as quickly as possible. As a result, Hitler could be certain that he would not have to fight on two fronts if an

Concentration camp inmates. The fate of innumerable former inmates can be read in the heaps of 'spare' clothes and shoes.

Secret clauses provided for a Russo-German partition of Poland in the event of war.

Ultimatum: notice of final terms which must be complied with if war is to be avoided.

See page 42.

attack on Poland brought Britain and France to declare war. The reason for this haste was that the last feasible date for an attack on Poland was 2 September, when an offensive would have time to crash through before the autumn rains bogged down the German armour. The Russo-German agreement left a few days to spare for a possible 'Munich' at the end of August, but was clearly designed with war in mind.

When Hitler's final diplomatic move failed to elicit a satisfactory Polish response, a number of Polish cross-border 'attacks' were staged, and German troops began an offensive on 1 September 1939. On 3 September, first Britain and then France issued an ultimatum demanding a German withdrawal; and the Germans' failure to answer meant that a European war had broken out.

Looking at Hitler's foreign policies during the 1930s, what seems most striking is the speed at which he operated. Within a single year (March 1938-March 1939) he won more territory without fighting than most great powers acquire through centuries of diplomacy. But speedy repetition in one crisis after another made his methods obvious – the threats and bullying, above all the lie that his latest diplomatic onslaught represented his 'final territorial demand in Europe'. So Hitler's diplomatic credibility diminished, and statesmen of other nations who were reluctant to fight eventually became convinced that they would have no choice.

Why the hurry? Some of the obvious answers are that Hitler was intoxicated by action, contemptuous of the 'decadent' statesmen who sought to placate him, and insatiably greedy for power. But there were also less personal reasons. There was the orientation of the German economy, discussed earlier, and the militarized ethos of the Third Reich, which appeared to require large doses of 'heroic action'. And there was a fear that the political and military situation would never again be so favourable: with Britain, France and Russia rearming, time might be running out for Germany.

Historians who believe in large impersonal forces emphasize such factors. Others give more weight to Hitler's personal traits – not only his craving for power, but also his fear that he might be dying of cancer or might be assassinated, in which case Germany would be deprived of the one man who could fulfil her destiny. 'All depends on me, on my existence, because of my political talents . . . . No one knows how much longer I shall live. Therefore, better a conflict now.' This was what Hitler told the senior commanders of the armed forces on 22 August 1939, when he was

Rationalizations: reasons put forward to justify actions which are in fact non-rational in origin.

preparing for the outbreak of war. Interestingly, he also put forward all the economic and political considerations mentioned above, leaving subsequent generations the task of distinguishing between 'real' reasons and rationalizations – if that can possibly be done.

The War Lord

Hitler at war: bungler or genius?

During a war that lasted almost six years, Hitler took innumerable decisions. It is obviously not possible to discuss them all in a book of this size, or even to cover every theatre of the war. But we can try to pick out certain patterns of behaviour, and register some of the judgements that have been made about the nature and quality of Hitler's leadership in war.

For a long time there was general agreement about this:

> Until fairly recently it was fashionable to dismiss Hitler as a bungling amateur in military matters, the opinionated corporal of the First World War, utterly out of his depth as a supreme commander, a carpet-biting maniac even, who pulled Germany down to defeat through his wholly irrational conduct of the war. This view of Hitler rests very largely on the testimony of certain German generals who rushed into print after the war and blamed the Führer, conveniently deceased, for all that had gone wrong after 1942 while carefully claiming credit, on behalf of the army, for Germany's earlier successes.
> Carr, *Hitler*

Now, as Carr goes on to say, 'a more accurate and historically credible picture is emerging'. But the older attitudes die surprisingly hard, doubtless because Hitler was a hateful man and it is psychologically more satisfying to denigrate his every action. As recently as 1984, an entire book was devoted to his supposed errors. In it, he is written off as a waverer who should have invaded Britain in 1940, should have ignored Franco's refusal to let German troops march through Spain against British-held Gibraltar, should have concentrated the entire German effort in 1941 on taking Moscow; and so on – at such length that it becomes difficult to understand how on earth Germany managed to fight on for so long.

Franco: Spanish dictator whom Hitler and Mussolini had helped during the Spanish Civil War (1936-9).

This kind of exercise is undermined by the fact that military historians disagree with one another concerning some aspect of every decision – inevitably so, since might-have-beens are always difficult to evaluate, and never more so than in the heightened circumstances of war. In other words, it is not so easy to put Hitler (or Churchill or Stalin) 'right': many big decisions include a substanial element of guesswork or intuition, and are not easily evaluated even with the benefit of hindsight.

A more modest approach to Hitler's war leadership might begin with the qualities he undoubtedly showed in conferences – his excellent grasp of strategy and tactics, his wide technical knowledge and extremely powerful memory. It might also note that a good many competent military men were impressed by him, some of them even after the end of the Third Reich had removed any self-interested motives for expressing admiration. Then, having established that Hitler was a commander worth taking seriously – *not* that he was necessarily a genius – it should be possible to examine his successes and failures, asking whether they derived from his talents, his temperament, his outlook on the world, or other factors.

Hitler played little part in the rapid defeat of Poland, although France's failure to aid her ally confirmed his judgement that Germany would not be compelled to fight on two fronts. But he was primarily responsible for the main plan leading to the conquest of Norway in April 1940, and for the crucial decision that defeated France in May: to draw the Allied armies forward by a secondary attack through the Low Countries, and then to launch the main attack through the Ardennes. If Hitler did not originate this last plan (which was suggested by General Erich von Manstein), he did take it up and make it his own, in opposition to the conventional operations proposed by the high command. This can be interpreted as a proof of Hitler's military insight; but it can also be argued that it was more a matter of temperament: Hitler's entire career shows his preference for the sudden, unexpected thrust that threw his opponents off balance, defeating them morally as well as materially.

Could this be true of most decision-making?

France followed the pattern, collapsing within six weeks. There seems little doubt that this stunning victory – his first over a great power – had a profound effect on Hitler. It convinced him that he was a military genius, and justified his contempt for the senior German generals. This was partly a matter of social prejudice, for they distrusted the vulgar upstart corporal, while he resented and was made uncomfortable by their socially exclusive backgrounds. But they had also opposed him at almost every turn, arguing that a march into the Rhineland was too risky, contemplating the arrest of Hitler if war broke out against Czechoslovakia, and even slowing down the production of the armour that Hitler rightly saw as the key to a new Blitzkrieg style of warfare.

Blitzkrieg: the 'lightning warfare', waged with tanks and other armoured vehicles backed by aeroplane strikes etc., that gave Hitler and Germany their greatest victories.

Events seemed to prove that, on every occasion, Hitler had been right and his generals wrong. After the defeat of France it would be a long time before they could think of opposing him again. Meanwhile with this victory he had become 'the infallible Führer', much less inclined to seek advice or tolerate contradiction; so that when the setbacks began, he would assume that the blame must lie with his subordinates, and his distrust and suspicion of the generals became even more violent.

But this was not yet apparent on 22 June 1941, when the German armies launched an all-out, unprovoked attack on the Soviet Union. It was true that Britain was unsubdued, and that the 'Battle of Britain' in the air had gone against the Luftwaffe; but the British were hardly in a position to invade the Continent even when three million Axis soldiers were engaged in the East. Nevertheless the invasion of the USSR has understandably been called Hitler's fatal mistake. The entire war hinged on it – by comparison, the campaigns in North Africa and Italy were negligable affairs, and even the Allies' landings in Normandy were secondary. The fate of Hitler and Nazi Germany – and therefore of Europe – was decided in this vast and savage conflict.

See page 50.

It is tempting to argue that Hitler should have consolidated his grip on continental Europe, especially since Stalin was dutifully carrying out the terms of the 1939 non-aggression pact by supplying Germany with wheat, oil and other vital materials. But if Hitler had been a consolidator, rather than a 'plunger' and a man in a hurry, he would never have acquired his continental empire in the first place: in that sense his career is all of a piece, and he could hardly be expected to stop short at the conquest named in *Mein Kampf* as the ultimate prize. Moreover, it would be easy. The Soviet army was in disarray after Stalin's purges, and its poor quality seemed evident from its mediocre performance against little Finland in 1940. The army that had defeated France in six weeks could surely make short work of a demoralized Bolshevik rabble. Hitler was not the only person to think so:

Although he claimed to fear a possible Russian 'stab in the back', Hitler was probably more influenced by his ingrained anti-Bolshevism, his preoccupation with living-space and the tempting prospect of not having to pay for his wheat and oil. Does the evidence indicate that sheer lust for conquest should be added to the list?

Practically all qualified judges thought that fighting would be over within a few

CIGS: Chief of the Imperial General Staff.

weeks. No German general expressed doubts as some had done before the invasion of France. British Intelligence gave the Russians ten days. Cripps, the British Ambassador in Moscow, said a month. Dill, the CIGS, thought the Russians might last six weeks. In America Roosevelt's military advisers told him, 'Germany will be fully occupied in beating Russia for a minimum of one month and a possible maximum of three.'
A.J.P. Taylor, *The Second World War: an illustrated history*, Hamish Hamilton, 1975.

So ideology, economics, egomania and military advantage all favoured an early attack. However repulsive the framework within which Hitler's thinking was done, the thinking itself cannot be so easily faulted.

Hitler and his generals shared this assumption.

All German planning was based on the assumption that an early victory would make it unnecessary for the army to endure 'General Winter', supposedly the 'secret weapon' that had defeated Napoleon during *his* invasion of Russia in 1812. But although the German offensive took the Russians by surprise and inflicted enormous losses on them, the vast distances and dogged resistance slowed the German advance. Here too there are widely different opinions about the wisdom of Hitler's decisions – and the fact that experts disagree can be taken to prove, at the very least, that he was not 'bungling'. Finally, in December 1941, German forces glimpsed the golden domes of Moscow, only to be faced with their first major shock – not the Russian winter, unwelcome though that was, but the counter-offensive launched on 6 December by a supposedly broken Soviet army. The consequent crisis brought Hitler to the height of his power: on 16 December he issued a 'stand fast' order forbidding any retreat, and took over personal command of the German armies. Most historians think that Hitler's stand fast order prevented a calamitous rout of the kind suffered by Napoleon's Grand Army, and was therefore justified despite the cost in German lives – though it should be added that an orderly withdrawal would have been possible if Hitler or his generals had thought to prepare positions to fall back on.

Which is not in fact the same as saying that the war was lost.

It has often been claimed that Hitler now knew that the war was lost; much has been made, for example, of his remark to General Jodl that 'victory can no longer be achieved'. But it seems more probable that this was a passing fit of gloom. The following year the prospects for victory again seemed excellent, as Hitler's table talk (private conversations taken down by a stenographer) indicated. At the end of February 1942 he said:

I can tell you now that during the first two weeks of December we lost a thousand tanks and had two thousand locomotives out of operation . . . . Now, when I send something to the southern sector, I know that it will reach its destination. We have nothing more to fear from climatic mishaps.
   Now that January and February are over, our enemies can give up hope of our suffering the fate of Napoleon. . . . Now we're about to switch over to squaring the account. What a relief!
Hitler's Table Talk 1941-44, Weidenfeld, 1953.

Of course it is possible to believe that Hitler was secretly convinced that it was all over; and one writer even claims that he was determined to hang on as long as possible in order to exterminate the Jews:

In December 1941 Hitler the politician finally abdicated in favour of Hitler the mass murderer.
Sebastian Haffner, *The Meaning of Hitler*, Weidenfeld, 1979.

The only real evidence for this is the coincidence of dates – the Russian counter-offensive and Hitler's declaration of war on the USA in December

1941, followed by the organization of systematic extermination in January 1942. The reader must judge whether or not this is a plausible interpretation.

Historians have been at a loss to explain Hitler's declaration of war on the United States, which followed the devastating Japanese attack on Pearl Harbor on 7 December 1941. It is true that Japan was allied to Germany and Italy; but they were only obliged to come to her aid if she was the party that had been attacked. It is also true that, although technically neutral, the United States was Germany's enemy, giving so much covert aid to Britain that something like an undeclared state of war already existed in the Atlantic. But a war in the Pacific might have persuaded the Americans to keep the peace with Germany; and Hitler had nothing much to lose by following a wait-and-see policy. It is hard to interpret his declaration as anything but an outburst of resentment or irritation, or else a wild operatic surrender to the prospect of setting the world ablaze – luxuries Hitler had previously denied himself whenever there were strong practical reasons.

The mass murderer

No question mark is needed after this heading: the evidence for Hitler's mass murders is overwhelming. His racial obsessions and his vision of life as a ruthless struggle for mastery found expression before the war in persecutions and brutalities, in the setting up of concentration camps where 'enemies of the state' were maltreated, and in an unscrupulous foreign policy based on lies and force. But it was only after the attack on Poland that the mass murders began, mainly but not exclusively carried out by Heinrich Himmler's black-uniformed SS, which expanded so quickly that it became a state within the state.

A bare listing is sufficient to convey the scope of these horrors. On the outbreak of war Hitler signed an order for the killing of incurables, the mentally disabled and other *German* 'useless eaters', about 100,000 of whom perished. After the conquest of Poland, a determined effort was made to destroy the country's political, social and cultural elite (perhaps a million people); the masses were to be denied any but the most elementary education so that the existence of the Poles would be reduced to the most primitive level. A similar policy was followed in German-occupied Russia, where commissars and other leading personnel were routinely murdered. Moreover millions of Russian prisoners of war were starved to death in camps or worked to death in German factories.

So the Jews were by no means the only victims. What distinguishes them – and also the gypsies – is that an attempt was made literally to exterminate them. In the early stages of the war, huge numbers in Poland and Russia were shot and buried in mass graves which they had been forced to dig

This gave rise to the completely unfounded belief that Germany and Japan worked closely together before and during the war, and even that Hitler masterminded Pearl Harbor!

Commissars: in the USSR, Communist Party officials charged with political education duties, especially when attached to the Red Army.

This is generally described as genocide – race murder.

Hitler and Mussolini contemplate the wreckage after the unsuccessful attempt on Hitler's life of 20 July 1944.

before being executed. But from 1942 special 'death camps' were set up, equipped with large gas chambers and crematoria, so that the murdering could be turned into a production-line process; and the Nazis extended the scope of their activities, transporting Jews from all over Europe to Auschwitz, Treblinka and other death camps in the east. This was the Holocaust, in which millions perished. (Neo-Nazis have sometimes tried to dismiss the existence of death camps as a myth by pointing out, correctly, that such notorious places as Belsen and Dachau had no gas chambers. But these camps in Germany were concentration camps – vile enough places, but not specially equipped for mass extermination.)

These acts of organized insanity could be called doubly mad, since most of them actually hindered the German war effort. There may have been a sinister logic in using slave labour to keep Germany's factories going, which freed men for war service; but transporting and killing Jews constituted an enormous waste of men and resources, and the atrocities committed on Soviet territory were even less prudent, alienating the Ukranians and other nationalities who had originally welcomed the Germans as liberators. It is at least possible that these crimes made the difference between victory and defeat; and the fact that they were committed in the middle of a life-and-death struggle is surely the final proof that Hitler genuinely believed in his own grotesque visions. His timing in realizing the visions can be seen as a 'natural' culmination of his life's purposes, or as a final slide into megalomania.

Only one historian has challenged the commonly received version of Hitler's wartime crimes. In *Hitler's War* (1977) and *The War Path* (1978) David Irving argues that Hitler did not order the annihilation of the Jews and was probably unaware that it was happening. On this view, Himmler was the race fanatic, acting on his own responsibility – by contrast with Hitler, who had cynically used anti-semitism as a vote-catcher, 'riding that evil horse right up to the portals of the Chancellery in 1933'. According to Irving, Nazi anti-semitic measures before the war represented concessions to Party opinion or, like Crystal Night, were launched against Hitler's wishes and were put an end to by him. The main wartime evidence offered by Irving is the absence of any written order by Hitler for the elimination of the Jews, and Himmler's scribbled record of a telephone conversation, 'Jewish transport from Berlin, no liquidation'.

Here it is impossible to do justice to the arguments on either side, which depend on the evaluation of many kinds of evidence. Irving's playing down of Hitler's anti-semitism seems the weakest part of his argument, sustainable only by dismissing as unreliable a variety of source materials which all point in the same direction, and by regarding the appalling utterances of a lifetime as no more than coolly calculated propaganda. Moreover the telephone conversation is ambiguous as well as slender evidence, since Hitler's veto can be taken to imply that he was closely involved in the deportations and liquidations. But the lack of a written order is striking – especially since, as Irving points out, such orders *were* issued for the other mass murders described earlier. Irving's critics have countered by suggesting that an order was unnecessary because the entire Holocaust was an internal (Nazi/SS) matter, and that documentation was kept to a minimum because the truth had to be kept from the German people as well as the world at large. Quotations and counter-quotations have been flung to and fro without entirely clarifying the issue. It is only fair to Irving to state his basic contention, that

of explicit, wartime evidence, the kind of evidence that could hang a man, not one line has been produced

Holocaust (fiery destruction) has become a widely used term to describe the Nazis' murder of 4-6 million Jews.

Megalomania: insane delusion of greatness or omnipotence.

The death camps were outside Germany, far to the east. This suggests that the Nazification of ordinary Germans was far from complete.

before noting that almost all other historians have found the notion that such a vast operation could take place without Hitler's knowledge – and without one of Himmler's jealous rivals informing on him – utterly incredible.

An interesting feature of the controversy is that it actually has no great moral significance: even if Irving is right, Hitler would still be self-condemned as a mass murderer on the basis of the orders he did sign. And in fact Irving's case is intended to support a different line of argument, – 'that Hitler was a less omnipotent Führer than has been believed'. The indignation aroused by Irving's books demonstrates that, after all these years, Hitler's reputation remains an extraordinarily emotive subject.

Is there evidence anywhere else in this book to support such an assertion?

The end of a madman?

As the 'Final Solution' – the Holocaust – took shape early in 1942, the Axis reached the height of its good fortune. Rommel won impressive victories in North Africa, German U-boats took a heavy toll of Allied shipping in the Atlantic, and Japan conquered much of South-East Asia. In the decisive Eastern sector, German armies thrust towards the twin objectives of Stalingrad and the Caucasian oilfields, winning new victories that convinced both Hitler and his generals that the Russians were finished.

Then in the second half of 1942 the tide began to turn. The Germans and Italians were driven from North Africa. In February 1943, after a titanic battle for the city, the German Sixth Army surrendered at Stalingrad. In spite of this catastrophe the Germans mounted a new offensive, only to suffer a shattering defeat at Kursk in July 1943. From this point it was clear that the Russians were winning. Meanwhile the Battle of the Atlantic had been lost and the industrial strength as well as the manpower of the United States was increasingly felt. Allied forces invaded Italy, which changed sides after the fall of Mussolini, creating another front for the Germans to defend. When the Allies' landings in Normandy proved successful in June 1944, it was obviously only a matter of time before Germany was squeezed to death. A group of German conspirators, most of them military men, recognized as much and planned to assassinate Hitler, overthrow the Third Reich, and negotiate a peace. But the Bomb Plot of 20 July 1944 failed to kill Hitler, for whose hopeless cause Germany fought on until May 1945.

The Battle of the Atlantic involved a protracted German attempt to destroy Allied convoys by submarine (U-boat) warfare. Although the U-boats inflicted enormous material losses, they were eventually mastered.

The Hitler of these years is generally pictured as becoming steadily less rational in his demands on his generals, more prone to error and increasingly remote from realities. There is certainly evidence that his powers deteriorated. During the war he tended to avoid contact with the population, spending most of his time shut off in a fortified headquarters – the Wolf's Lair (Wolfsschanze) in East Prussia, at Vinnitsa in the Ukraine

After the Bomb Plot: Hitler, holding steady his damaged arm, confers with other survivors. The man behind him is Martin Bormann, who used his position as Hitler's secretary to acquire considerable power in the final years of the Third Reich. A terrible vengeance was wreaked on the plotters.

Among the ruins of the Reich: British troops parade beside the Brandenburg Gate in Berlin.

during the decisive period of the Russian campaign, and finally, as things fell apart, in the bunker below his own Reich Chancellery in Berlin, where he took his life. Convinced that only he could take the right decisions – contemptuous as well as distrustful of his generals – Hitler worked ceaselessly in a vain attempt to control the conduct of the war in detail. Albert Speer, his armaments minister noted that

Overwork and isolation led to a peculiar state of petrifaction and rigor. He suffered from spells of mental torpor and was permanently caustic and irritable. Earlier, he had made decisions with almost sportive ease; now, he had to force them out of his exhausted brain.
Albert Speer, *Inside the Third Reich*, Weidenfeld, 1970.

Speer believed that overwork impeded Hitler's decision-making by depriving him of the long reflective 'holiday' periods during which he had earlier conceived some of his most effective plans. And while overwork sapped Hitler's judgement, his insistence on detailed control of operations was often counter-productive, making local commanders dangerously dependent on tardy instructions from on high. To give only one example: immediately after the first Normandy landings, significant decisions had to be delayed while the news was telephoned to Berchtesgaden, from which Hitler thereafter insisted on directing the vital effort to destroy the Allied beachhead.

Overworked and overwrought, Hitler was also increasingly a sick man and – perhaps more important – a man pumped full of drugs by his physician, Dr Theodor Morell. After being injured in the Bomb Plot of 20 July 1944 he was in even worse shape, his right arm trembling uncontrollably and his walk reduced to an old man's shuffle. Photographs provide irrefutable evidence of his physical deterioration.

However, Franklin D. Roosevelt ran America's war from a wheelchair, and Hitler's ailments may not have made any fundamental difference to his conduct of the war. In fact it can be argued that his behaviour pattern changed remarkably little: in both peace and war he favoured two modes of operation: the daring unexpected stroke when he was the attacker, and the tenacious, unyielding stand in defence. The 'stand fast' order reflected his conviction that miracles could be achieved by sheer will-power. It had saved the situation in December 1941, but when Hitler repeated it again and again, in ever more unfavourable circumstances, his refusal to allow strategic retreats, or a straightening of a defensive line, was responsible for huge German losses. So it can be argued that Hitler's 'brilliant' order of December 1941 and his 'insane' later orders sprang from the same

For example he had 'stood fast' in late 1932 (see page 33).

fundamental impulses or reactions. Could it be that such impulses (rather than calculations) play a larger role in decision-making than is generally realized – and that a leader remains a 'genius' only so long as his impulses happen to correspond with realities?

Hitler's audacities were not much in evidence during the later stages of the war; perhaps, as Speer suggested, he was too mentally fatigued, or perhaps the worsening situation inhibited him. But on occasion he could still react promptly to crises, ordering German troops to take control in Vichy France (November 1942) and Italy (September 1943) when these satellites seemed likely to fall to the Allies, and securing the rescue of his fallen ally and fellow-dictator Mussolini. Characteristically, Hitler was disappointed by Mussolini's lack of interest in wreaking a terrible revenge on the former friends who had brought him down.

There are other indications that Hitler's deterioration was far from complete. To the very end he inspired many people whom he interviewed with a renewed confidence in final victory. And as late as December 1944 he was able to conceive and impose on his unwilling generals 'the Battle of the Bulge' – an offensive thrust in the West that was very much in his old audacious vein. But the balance of forces was now too one-sided for the offensive to have any serious prospect of success: again, it was not so much the man as the circumstances that had altered. Or as A.J.P. Taylor puts it,

> This was Hitler's last gamble – brilliant in conception, impossible to execute. The God of War does not love cleverness; he loves the Big Battalion.
> A.J.P. Taylor, *The Second World War*, Hamish Hamilton, 1975.

By this time the situation was utterly hopeless, and a different kind of leader might have spared his people needless suffering. Instead, Hitler and his entourage grasped at straws. High hopes were placed in secret weapons such as the new jets, for which there was no longer enough fuel. And, failing that, there was the conviction that the 'unnatural' partnership between Britain, the USA and Communist Russia must break down. It was a matter of keeping one's nerve ('stand fast' again). When President Roosevelt died on 12 April 1945, Hitler and Goebbels rejoiced: had not the old Prussian king, Frederick the Great, been saved by the death of the Russian Empress Catherine, whose successor changed sides? But that fantasy faded when Roosevelt's successor showed no signs of following suit.

Meanwhile Hitler tried to impose a 'scorched earth' policy on Germany, ordering mass immigration into the interior and the destruction of all industrial and other resources that might be of use to the advancing enemy. No doubt this was partly a way of revenging himself on the German people, who had failed him; and no doubt his imagination responded to the prospect of bringing a continent down in ruins with him. But prolonging the war by any means was also consistent with his belief in ruthless racial struggle, which told him that, if defeated, the Germans would in any case be enslaved or exterminated. To put it another way, he judged others by himself. He told Speer 'in an icy tone' that

> If the war is lost, the people will be lost also. It is not necessary to worry about what the German people will need for elemental survival. On the contrary, it is best for us to destroy even these things. For the nation has proved to be the weaker, and the future belongs solely to the stronger eastern nation. In any case only those who are inferior will remain after this struggle, for the good have already been killed.
> Speer, *Inside the Third Reich*.

If this can be called madness, it was a madness described in the pages of

---

Vichy France: the part of France not occupied by the Germans. Vichy was its capital.

All the more remarkable in that such confidence was, of course, entirely irrational.

The Allies also helped to prolong the war by their 1943 declaration that they would accept nothing short of unconditional surrender.

An unreal, claustrophobic atmosphere prevailed in the Berlin bunker during the last weeks of the Third Reich; see H.R. Trevor-Roper's definitive *Last Days of Hitler*. However, Hitler's suicide was a rational decision; it was his followers – intriguing for non-existent political advantages after his death – who behaved in a fashion that might be labelled insane.

Mein Kampf and present throughout Hitler's political life.

Fortunately for Germany, Speer and others disobeyed and averted the worst. As the Russians closed in on Berlin, Hitler decided to die in the city. On 29 April 1945 he married his companion of many years, Eva Braun; the following day they retired to their private quarters, where she took poison and Hitler shot himself.

Conclusions

At the end of such an argumentative book, readers should perhaps be left to draw their own conclusions. Various alternative interpretations of Hitler's personality and career have been presented here with some attempt at fairness – to the interpretations, and even to Hitler himself. But of course the present writer's own convictions are pretty visible: that despite Hitler's violent personality and repulsive view of the world he was a man whose abilities it is foolish to deny – morally mad, perhaps, rather than clinically so; and that he was extraordinarily fixed and consistent in temperament, outlook, aims and preferred method. On this view, it was not Hitler who changed so much as the realities which he sought to dominate.

Two more issues are worth raising. Would the course of history have been significantly different if Hitler had not been born, or had been assassinated at any one of several points in his career? The debate concerning the individual's role in history is an old one, but in the case of a conqueror-despot such as Hitler, it is especially acute. Was he, for all his charisma and seemingly unlimited power, no more than the agent of (say) German capitalism or a tendency towards expansion that was inevitable because of Germany's economic and geographical position? An investigation of this fundamental historical issue is beyond the scope of this book, but is well worth pursuing.

Finally, was Hitler a great man? Of course the answer depends on what we mean by 'great'. In ordinary usage it includes an element of admiration, grudging or otherwise – an admiration readily extended to figures such as Queen Elizabeth I or Napoleon Bonaparte, whose attractive qualities are recognized in spite of their responsibility for a number of political murders. But the main component in greatness (as we ordinarily use the word) is the sheer impact made on the world by the individual in question.

With Hitler, however, matters are not so simple. His powerful but narrow, hate-filled personality repels; and the murders – so many millions of them – stifle the sense of excitement normally aroused by conflicts and conquests on the grand scale, even when our minds disapprove of them. Yet if greatness is finally a matter of moving and astonishing the world, there is no escaping the fact that Hitler *was* a great man. Alternatively, we might begin to grow up, and to revise our ideas about what constitutes true greatness.

Hitler's Contemporaries

Chamberlain, Neville (1868-1940). British Prime Minister 1937-40; negotiated with Hitler and signed Munich agreement to appease him 1938. Reluctantly led Britain into war 1939.

Churchill, Winston (1874-1965). British politician, at various times Home Secretary and Chancellor of the Exchequer. Out of office in 1930s, repeatedly warned of Hitler menace. Proved right, he became Prime Minister 1940 and led Britain through the war. Defeated in 1945 election, but again Prime Minister 1951-55.

Einstein, Albert (1879-1955). German-born physicist whose theory of relativity revolutionized ideas about the universe. As a Jew, left Germany after Nazis took power in 1933, settling in the USA.

Franco, Francisco (1892-1975). Spanish general, led revolt against elected government 1936 and won Spanish Civil War 1936-9 with German and Italian help. His semi-fascist dictatorship lasted until his death.

Goebbels, Dr Joseph (1897-1945). Nazi propaganda chief during the party's rise to power. Minister of National Enlightenment and Propaganda 1933-45. Small, lame, a cynical manipulator. Remained with Hitler in the Berlin bunker, killing his family and himself.

Göring, Hermann (1893-1946). Leading Nazi, fighter ace during First World War. Fat and apparently jovial, but ruthless and able. Wounded in 1923 Putsch. Played key role in consolidation of Nazi power after 1933. Put in charge of German economy and built up Luftwaffe (air force), whose failure in 1940 contributed to decline in Göring's prestige during war. Surrendered and put on trial for war crimes 1945; sentenced to death but took poison.

Hess, Rudolf (1894-1987). Leading Nazi. Took down *Mein Kampf* from Hitler's dictation in prison 1923. Deputy party leader and second in succession (behind Göring) as head of state 1939. Flew to Scotland in attempt to make peace with Britain 1941. Imprisoned for rest of war and, despite doubts about his sanity, condemned to life imprisonment – which was served in full.

Hindenburg, Paul von (1847-1934). German commander whose major victories and activities as Chief of German Staff in First World War gave him enormous prestige. Elected President of the Weimar Republic 1925. Re-elected, defeating Hitler, 1931, but persuaded by trusted conservative advisers to appoint Hitler as Chancellor 1933.

Hugenberg, Alfred (1865-1951). German politician, leader of Nationalist Party 1928-33; also controlled huge newspaper and film empire. Minister in first Hitler cabinet January 1933, but dissolved his party and resigned in same year.

Ludendorff, Erich (1865-1937). General, most famous German soldier of First World War after Hindenburg (*see above*). Took part in 1923 Putsch, but later broke with Hitler, becoming increasingly eccentric in ideas.

Mosley, Sir Oswald (1896-1980). British politician. After career as Conservative and Labour MP, founded British Union of Fascists 1932. Despite spectacular rallies and marches, and attempts to exploit anti-semitism, attracted only limited following. Interned as possible security risk 1940-43. His post-war Union Movement was a failure.

Mussolini, Benito (1883-45). Italian Fascist leader. Prominent socialist journalist until 1915; founded Fascist Party 1919; became Prime Minister 1922, gradually transforming Italy into a totalitarian state with himself as 'Duce' (Leader). Initially hostile to Hitler, but their common wish to expand brought them together in the face of the democracies' opposition. Conquered Abyssinia 1935, Albania 1939. Remained neutral in Second World War until German victories induced him to declare war on France 1940. Invaded Greece 1940, but defeats there and in North Africa revealed Italian weakness. After Allied invasion of Italy, forced to resign and imprisoned July 1943, but rescued by Germans. Captured and shot by Italian partisans.

Papen, Franz von (1879-1969). German conservative politician, Chancellor May-November 1932. To regain power, organized new government 1933 in which he served as Vice-Chancellor, mistakenly believing he could control Chancellor Adolf Hitler. From 1934 relegated to diplomatic posts; acquitted of major war crimes 1946.

Röhm, Ernst (1887-1934). Leading Nazi, a professional soldier who took part in the 1923 Putsch. From 1931 commander of SA (stormtroopers), for whom he planned an independent role in the Nazi state. As a result, shot during the Night of the Long Knives.

Roosevelt, Franklin D. (1882-1945). US President 1933-45. Launched 'New Deal' to combat economic depression. Hostile to Fascism, opposed Japanese expansion and, despite US neutrality, aided British against Germany. Japanese attack on Pearl Harbor brought USA into Second World War December 1941. Died in April 1945, shortly before victory.

Schuschnigg, Kurt von (1897-1977). Austrian politician, chancellor with dictatorial powers 1934-8, until Nazi pressure forced union with Germany. In custody until liberated by Allies 1945.

Speer, Albert (1905-81). German architect who became one of Hitler's intimates and, as armaments minister, galvanized the Nazi war effort. Imprisoned for war crimes 1946-66, Speer became the most articulately repentant of the leading Nazis, vividly describing the regime in books such as *Inside the Third Reich.*

Stalin, Joseph (1879-1953). Soviet leader, virtual dictator from about 1928, whose rule was accompanied by rapid industrialization, collectivization of agriculture and purges, at an appalling cost in human life. In search of security, agreed to a non-aggression pact with Nazi Germany 1939, but taken by surprise when Germans attacked 1941. Led USSR to victory and control of Eastern Europe; remained all-powerful until death.

Strasser, Gregor (1892-1934). Nazi leader, representing the more radical north German wing of the party. Often in conflict with Hitler, he resigned in 1932. Although not linked with Röhm (*see above*), Strasser was murdered during the Night of the Long Knives.

Stresemann, Gustav (1878-1929). German Chancellor 1923 and Foreign Minister 1923-9, worked for rehabilitation of Germany (admitted to League of Nations 1926) and reconciliation with former enemies (Locarno Pact 1925). Nobel Peace Prize 1926.

Book List

Bell, P.M.H., *The Origins of the Second World War in Europe*, Longman paperback, 1986.

Bullock, Alan, *Hitler: a study in tyranny*, Odhams, 1952; revised paperback edition, Pelican, 1962.

Carr, William, *Hitler: a study in personality and politics*, Arnold, 1978; paperback, 1986.

Churchill, Winston S., *Great Contemporaries*, Macmillan, 1937.

Churchill, Winston S., *The Second World War*, Cassell, 6 vols, 1948-54; various subsequent editions.

Fest, Joachim C., *Hitler*, Weidenfeld, 1974; paperback, 1987.

Hitler, Adolf, *Mein Kampf* (Ralph Mannheim translation), Hutchinson, 1969; paperback, 1974.

Hitler's Table Talk, Weidenfeld, 1953; Longman paperback, 1986.

Irving, David, *Hitler's War*, Michael Joseph, 1977.

Irving, David, *The War Path*, Michael Joseph, 1978.

Koch, H.W.(ed), *Aspects of the Third Reich*, Macmillan paperback, 1985.

Lewin, Ronald, *Hitler's Mistakes*, Leo Cooper/Secker, 1984.

Mann, Golo, *The History of Germany since 1789*, Chatto, 1968; Pelican paperback, 1974.

Manvell, Roger, and Fraenkel, Heinrich, *The Hundred Days to Hitler*, Dent, 1974.

Shirer, William L., *The Rise and Fall of the Third Reich*, Secker, 1960; Pan paperback, 1964.

Speer, Albert, *Inside the Third Reich*, Weidenfeld, 1970; Sphere paperback, 1971.

Taylor, A.J.P., *The Origins of the Second World War*, Hamish Hamilton, 1961; Penguin paperback, 1964.

Taylor, A.J.P., *The Second World War*, Hamish Hamilton, 1975.

Trevor-Roper, H.R., *The Last Days of Hitler*, Macmillan, 1947. Pan paperback, revised edition, 1962.

Index